SPIRITUAL TRAVELER:

JOURNEYS BEYOND FEAR

A People's Guide to Basic Decency in International Relations

CAMERON POWERS

PUBLISHED BY G.L.DESIGN, BOULDER, CO

Spiritual Traveler: Journeys Beyond Fear, 1st Edition

Library of Congress Control Number: 2005923018
ISBN/SKU: 0-9745882-1-0
ISBN Complete: 978-0-9745882-1-6

Cover Design: Cameron Powers
All Photos taken by Kristina Sophia or Cameron Powers
unless otherwise noted.

Contents:

Preface: The Limits of Compassion   1
Prologue: The Magic of Distant Realms   3

Seven Billion People: Seven Billion Points of View   7
1) Everyone is Always Right from his or her own Point of View   9
2) Is English the Only Language in which it is Possible to be "Right?"   13
3) Do We Speak Language or does Language Speak Us?   17

Arabs, Tibetans, Americans, Chinese   25

Seeing People on the Street   35

Dealing with Fear   39
1) Reflections of Fear   41
2) Overcoming Fear: You are SAFER over There!   43
3) Fear of Learning Languages   49

Feeling Good   51
1) Sensuality and Music -- you Have to Feel Good Inside...   53
2) Sacred Flirtation   55
3) Musical Enlightenment and Ecstasy   59

Personal Mental Growth   61
1) Working against Arrogance -- sorry, it's not so easy...   63
2) 'Civilization' -- Whose?   69
3) Why Working for Peace is Not Enough   73

Personal Soul Growth   75
1) Gain a New Soul by Entering a New Culture   77
2) Enlightenment and Inner Peace -- in these times?   79
3) No Humor at the Expense of Others   81
4) Becoming the Prayer: No Fear   85
5) Worshipping the Feminine in the Middle East and Elsewhere   87
6) Study of Exotic Music: Middle Eastern Music as an Example   99
7) Becoming a Musical Ambassador   101
8) Learning to Become Responsible Global Citizens   105
9) Do we Really Want to Waste this Precious Lifetime?   107

Endnotes   108
Poem: "Tomatoes"   109
Recent Itinerary of Musical Missions   115

Preface

The Limits of Compassion

Look deeply into those eyes!
You are the person who is looking at you!
You are the being who is behind those eyes!

And you are you. But you are also George and Alice... and you are Ahmad and Rania... The horse is the rider and the rider is the horse.

Living consciousness is one being looking out through zillions of pairs of eyes... up to a point... up to what point? ...*up to a point where it hurts* and we withdraw into our individual consciousnesses and curtail our telepathy and our compassion.

We are not willing to still be that warm-eyed cow when it reaches the slaughter house. We are not willing to be soldiers in the army that just lost the battle. It's too painful.

If joy were the only sensation experienced by living beings, then we would have acknowledged eons ago that we are all one and simply rejoiced in the sharing. But no, joy is not the only sensation. Pain and fear claim their share of attention and none of us really want to show up for that. So much for cosmic consciousness. So much for telepathy. When the pain arrives we unplug, define our individual boundaries and silently breathe a sigh of relief that this time it's the other guy, the other gal, the other species doing the suffering.

A tinge of guilt remains. Somewhere we suspect that we tuned out of the shared mind when the going got rough. Now the truly human path is born. We are caught between courage and cowardice. We are caught between illumination and stubborn refusal and we fill in the space with lots of fabrications about why we just couldn't go for the whole ride. We invent blame, victimization and a thousand other soap opera themes to explain why our ecstatic connectedness dissolved when the suffering showed up.

However, the magnetism of enlightenment is still pulling on us. We know that all seven billion of us in the human species are in this together. We know that, circumstances of birth and fortune aside, we are all equally responsible for our common well-being. We know that we are all one.

We pick ourselves up, dust ourselves off and take another look. Yes, most of us survived the last few years; the last few moments... George and Alice, Ahmad and Rania are still here and they all have eyes and they all can look at you. The mystery deepens. You want to ask Ahmad if he's the same as you but human language is too slow, too clumsy for such questions. If we are to find this out, it will not be verbal explanations that bring the answers. It will be more of a silent knowing; a shared telepathy; a divine inspiration; some kind of intimate dance... we can't really describe this...

But here are the guidelines... here are the exercises... here are the practices... Thank you, dear one, for sharing this faith...

Singing with Palestinian Men
in Refugee Camp near Damascus, Syria

Prologue

The Magic of Distant Realms

The chapters which follow in this book stem from this musician's experiences with the celebration of life. I have become a "peace activist," motivated not so much by anger, as by ecstasy. We will look at using musical tools to further open channels of communication which are already there, but which we do not use consciously.

Being a musician I frequently wonder why I am even trying to use words, a relatively cumbersome medium compared to the sound-energy forms of music, to try and spread my excitement about life. But I have a logical mind too, as well as a musical soul. So here we go!

Life offers so much more, as the birds are telling us with their dancing flights and their early-morning singing, than the network of logical filters called language is capable of conveying. Yet language is our most powerful practical tool. It is also our greatest trap. But we will side-step the dangers and use it constructively. We will try and use language to demolish boundaries created by language! And we will try to use our adventures here on planet earth to deepen our spiritual awakening and live lives inspired by hope. The alternative, to make our choices out of fear, is not attractive.

Verbal eloquence was certainly not my strength early in life. I did not have the gift of persuasion which young friends of mine with quick tongues seemed to possess. I learned another way to communicate: I picked up my guitar and sang with passion about "John Henry, the 'steel-drivin' man," or about the presumably lost souls of unknown women who had worked at "The House of the Risin' Sun." People danced.

At age 21, I accepted an invitation to go on a mountaineering expedition to Peru. I became fascinated by the Inca people whom I found still alive and well in their Andean realm: all six million of them! I spent eight years learning their languages, Quechua and Spanish, and learning their music. I went back and forth between North and South America; I went in and out of anthropology and linguistics departments; I worked in mines in Colorado; I created "Cameron's Terrible Tours" and guided many young people through remote Andean villages. I lived in numerous communal settings in Colorado and New Mexico where I found myself surrounded by dancing people when I played. In Peru I somehow always seemed to be there for the four-day music and dance festivals which developed in small villages every time the cornerstone for a new house was laid and every time a child received a first haircut and every time dozens of other events created opportunity for celebration! The ecstatic energy was everywhere and it was bountiful. Later I had similar musical adventures in Greece, Mexico, Turkey, and finally, Egypt, Jordan, Syria, Lebanon and Iraq.

Several hundred villagers in central Egypt sang along with me in 1995 when I sang a well-known Egyptian song by Abd el Halim at an all-night outdoor party, and it struck me that I was actually performing the function of "ambassador." I was American; they were Egyptian. We didn't know much about each other.

Kristina and I found ourselves on the streets of Baghdad in mid-April of 2003. The US Marines had arrived in the city nine days earlier. We rode across the desert with an Iraqi driver after many warm sing-along send-offs from Jordanians who thought we had the right approach to being American Musical Ambassadors. Even the Jordanian soldiers who were "guarding" the border required of us a few songs each time we passed. These songs served to substitute for our lack of official papers. Jordanians, like most Arabs, are somewhat accustomed to living in the present. And amazing things always seem to happen here in the present. The Marines had their own vehicles and their own purposes. We didn't see much of them nor they of us although I did manage to show one of them my *oud*. "Wow! It's kind of like a fretless bass, huh?" he commented. I felt sad that the Marine Corps had not trained him to carry a musical instrument so that spare time between battles could be spent hanging out with "the enemy" learning and singing local popular songs.

In Baghdad, Kristina and I were singing songs which had been popular in Iraq at least since the 1930's. "We need to see more people like you!" an Iraqi man was jubilantly exclaiming to us while hugging me with delight. Again, I felt like a genuine ambassador. People looked at us: we were not wearing uniforms or carrying guns. We were carrying a musical instrument, an *oud*, and we were singing popular Arabic songs on street corners in Baghdad with whichever Iraqis cared to stop and sing… Another Iraqi man lovingly adjusted my eyebrows for me as I sang. Kristina led the vocals for the next song and then I passed my oud to an Iraqi musician in the crowd who treated us to another popular song.

We were transported into a street-corner, market-place world beyond fear and anger; beyond the symbolism of choosing between the "good guys" and the "bad guys…" We had been doing this on street corners in Jordan and the West Bank and Egypt for months and it was perfectly natural for us. The sound of gunfire around the corner and the smoke rising from the high-rise buildings was a dramatic tragedy. But it was a drama being played out by other players in another reality.

In October, 2003, Kristina and I were invited to sing before a crowd of 60,000 Egyptians in the Cairo Stadium to help raise funds for the creation of a children's cancer hospital. Tens of thousands of Egyptians sang along with us! There were also many Egyptian performers, but we were the only foreigners invited by the Egyptian fund-raising organization to perform on that day. This time we were on stages instead of street corners but it was the same for us. We, of course, sang popular Egyptian music.

We also call ourselves "Missionaries in Reverse." Everywhere we go we seek to learn from the ancient wisdoms of peoples and places. We have done concerts in a vast Palestinian refugee camp in Syria, and in Jordan, Lebanon and the West Bank. In all of these Arab-world cities we represented the "Compassionate Heart of America" and received constant encouragement by e-mail from thousands of Americans who wanted us to represent them.

Between November of 2002 and November of 2004 we gave over 170 concerts, presentations and workshops in both the Arab World and America.

Desiring to carry the images and songs from our Arab World concerts back to America, we began, in the summer of 2003, tours of the American West Coast, the South, the Pacific Northwest, the Western states, the Midwest and finally, the East Coast. We did this in an effort to neutralize the campaign of fear which we perceived to be coming from the American government and mainstream media. We were able to provide an up-lift for the ten thousand plus American citizens for whom we have done our presentations and we receive steady expressions of gratitude from American people who seem to be thirsting, perhaps even starving, for means of opening channels of communication with ordinary Arabs. There is a deep sense that Americans and Arab-world peoples are being railroaded into fearing each other even though there is no real basis for this. The horrific events of September 11, 2001 were orchestrated, we now know, by dissident members of high-level Saudi Arabian families who certainly don't represent the vast majority of Arab-speaking peoples. Yet it feels as though the dominant governmental decision-makers and media bosses are still doing more to sow suspicion and hatred than they are to fuel positive connections which could give people hope.

I am frightened that the modern obsession with making our world "safe" by force is causing people to forget that gentleness and generosity are the greatest guarantors of "safety."

Are we so obsessed with control that we have suffocated all the lovers? Are we so obsessed with "fighting for freedom" that we have forgotten how to simply be free?

In the process of "being on the road" for the last three years, Kristina and I have learned a lot about humanity: specifically about Arab-world humanity and American humanity. Learning to be able to listen carefully to what is said by other peoples in other languages requires our own personal presence in the here and now... And presence in the here and now is the only place where we can actually be... We have found that the path we have been following, called Musical Missions of Peace, continues to bring us out into the sunlight wherever we go. This book is an attempt to share some of the lessons we have learned "on the road." Where do we find some of the paths of ecstasy which unite us?

Hopefully, the only negative judgments made in this book are about making negative judgments! I use cultural examples from the Arab World to try and make it clear that the world can be viewed in many different ways. This is because of my recent fascination with the Arab World. I will have to leave it to someone else to write a similar book employing impressions gleaned from other cultures.

Special thanks go to Korkut Onaran, Brooke Anderson and Kristina Sophia for their critical help with proofing and revising this manuscript!

Seven Billion People: Seven Billion Points of View

Basic Orientation

Soaring on a breath of love, I fly high above my own mind.
I can see it grinding out my thoughts down below.
Semi-exhausted,
it staggers forward through the endless labyrinths of judgment:
"this is good and this is bad," it snarls for all to hear.
Up here there is no good and there is no evil.
There is only the blue of the sky, the green of the hills and the sounds of the
music!

Cairo, Egypt: what are this man's points of view?

Everyone is Always "Right"
From His or Her Own Point of View

We know that this is true. We must give up our own claim to being "more right" than others!

We have a right to expect others to realize that our own beliefs make sense to us, if not to them. And others have a right to expect the same from us. It is the habit of summarily dismissing others' beliefs as "wrong" that keeps getting us into trouble. A harmonious love relationship will probably not stay harmonious for long if both parties do not realize that each lover is always right from his or her own point of view. Initial attractions prevail for a long time, but sooner or later, the realization that one's beloved holds some different beliefs will need to be acknowledged. Slight differences can become magnified if space is not deliberately held open for their existence.

If you and your spouse and your friends are willing to hold each others' beliefs as sacred, the potential for divine laughter opens wide before you. Situations which can so easily be used to make other people "wrong," can suddenly just become funny. And the quality of your relationships at home is your springboard to your relationships with all others!

Cackling with crazy honking laughter, the wild geese pass overhead.
What is so funny?
Could it be that they have noticed what we people are doing?

Confrontational communication doesn't work very well. Each person feels sure about their own convictions the same way you feel sure about yours. People are more likely to adopt new beliefs when they feel that they are discovering things for themselves. To try to *persuade* someone or *prove* something to them usually has the opposite of the intended effect. They are stimulated to reinforce the beliefs they already hold rather than to expand them. Such is the negative effect of our typical attachment to "being right."

We must fly higher than we had ever suspected!
Flapping hard over the lands of all possibilities,
smooth breathing becomes a necessity.
"At last I have escaped being 'right'!
Flying higher, we at last pass behind the dark side of the moon.
When we see the earth again we will finally understand...

What is the most dangerous sort of person? Someone, obviously, who thinks that he, and he alone, is always right, or at the least, "more right" than others. This is a dangerously undemocratic position. I mentioned this simple truth to a newlywed bride not too long ago. She rolled her eyes, thinking of her new husband and about how "wrong" she knew him to be. Oh well, I guess this is where we all start from.

I received an e-mail not long ago from a pastor of a church. In response to my suggestion that the Islamic worlds and the Christian worlds might have things to learn from each other, he commented: "Our Lord says not to cast pearls before swine!" Oh well, I hope his world doesn't remain ruled by anger and fear and that his own discoveries made while following his own passion lead him out into a sunny place from where he can welcome all of humanity to sit equally at the same supper.

It takes some work to expand beyond our hometown communities. We seldom meet people with very different points of view from our own while we remain in our home communities. We have life-long habits of running in the same circles. We surround ourselves with like-minded people and come to regard the "others," whom we never even talk to, as hopelessly misguided. We even become afraid that we might run into one! How will we even talk with people so hopelessly wrong; so brain-washed?!

"Dad! Why do we blue parrots never even talk to the red parrots?"
"Well son, I'm not sure...
But I know that my parents never talked to one...
And I don't think my grandparents ever did either..."

And then it takes some more work to allow ourselves to hear others' points of view. And then still more work for us to truly realize that "we are all right from our own points of view." But there are some powerful forces which are, in fact, our allies.

FOLLOW THE FLOW OF LOVE

Trust the natural attractions which exist between all of us. These attractions will eventually lead us out into an ever-growing circle of beloved friends who will help us stretch ourselves. We are sometimes willing to consider a friend's point of view and eventually realize that it is "right."

It is when we adventure out and do some traveling and exploring that we actually begin to meet people with differing points of view. We are first struck by all the people we meet with whom we have so much in common. Eventually, we begin to hunger to meet those with whom we may not at first seem to have so much in common. We allow them to stretch us and then: amazing! ...we fall in love with a whole other dimension of humanity to which we had been previously closed! We begin to enjoy the "rightness" of other people and not just our own. Now this is real growth!

So, once we have broken out of our comfortable circles and begun meeting a wider variety of folks, what do we do? How can we open up to each other without making each other wrong from the start and thereby closing down communication?

This technique works: Everyone is compassionate in his or her own way. People love to have their own compassion acknowledged. If you meet someone with whom you feel you have nothing in common, find out where this person directs his or her compassion and see if you can share in that. Perhaps at first you find your own mind tending to make this person "wrong" because they seem to have political or religious beliefs opposed to your own. Then it is time to change the subject until you can find out where their compassion does flow. Perhaps, after some exploratory conversation, you discover that you are talking with a pigeon-lover devoted to eradicating all forms of pigeon abuse.

Then you must ask yourself: "Can I join this person in their sympathy for pigeons?"

If the answer is "yes," then jump right in. Allow your compassion to flow toward pigeons also! Remember that it's the flow of love that's important. As soon as your new friend senses the parallel compassion flowing through both of you toward pigeons, you will have a friend for life! Forget your own negative judgments and stay in the flow of love. Be thankful for each new person who gives you an opportunity to stretch the directions along which your *own* compassion can move!

Sooner or later we meet people who have advocated or been involved in violent behavior. While we may personally feel that we ourselves will never turn to violence, we may still need to understand what drives some people to commit violent acts. If we are to understand the whole spirit body of humanity, we must make this effort. After all is said and done, from an infinitely compassionate point of view, it does not even make sense to believe in "good" and "evil." Immerse a person in enough pain and he or she may do some strange things – not because he or she is "evil," but because he or she has ended up in some uniquely stressful situation. Ultimately, we all contain each other. If we had been born into someone else's shoes, we might have made their footprints! Through an open heart we learn to include and understand everyone.

Flying into the smoke...
We wonder why...?
We wonder who...?
Oh my God, they're real people too!
Why oh why oh why did I never listen to them before?
How was I to know
that it wasn't until I began hanging out
with "lost souls"
that I would discover my own?

These young Turkish folks couldn't stay seated after the band got warmed up. What does the world look like through their eyes?

Is English the Only Language in which it is Possible to be "Right?"

And what about all the folks who speak and think in dramatically different languages from ours? Chinese? Navajo? Arabic? They, too, are always right from their own points of view. It's amazing how many people don't even think about this. They may reach a point of giving speakers of their own language the benefit of all doubts, but it still never occurs to them that they must be prepared to do the same for all of humanity. And that this remains true even if we can't readily understand exactly what is being said!

What to do?
Depend on the local elected officials to solve this problem?
I don't think so...

Everyone is always "right" from his or her own point of view.
This is true no matter which language is being spoken.

Chinese people are "always right," just as Turkish people are "always right," just as Arab people are "always right," and so on... Quite an extensive exploration of the world is called for if we are to learn about who we all are!

Overwhelming? But think about it. What potential for personal growth! If we find ourselves hanging on to old worn-out patterns at home and having difficulty shedding them, then why not deliberately place ourselves where we absolutely must:
surrender our *expectations,*
place ourselves trustingly in the hands of whatever *higher powers* exist,
open every one of our *senses,*
learn to open every one of our *extra-senses,*
and become wide awake in *the present moment...?*

Gee, why doesn't everyone do this right now?

People talk about wanting to have transcendental experiences, but we are walking around in our own culture. And each culture is blind to the realities of other cultures. So we are going to have to make a personal effort. We need to get out of our home countries and live and move around in some other ones. It's funny though. There's this phenomenon called "tourism" which could make it possible for someone who just went to Egypt wonder on their way home if they *really* went to Egypt. And there are other ways, I think, for people in government and corporate environments to live in foreign countries without actually ever really arriving there.

But, for those who do choose to surrender to the people on planet earth and begin to wander among them, amazing paths are waiting!

Of course we must begin to learn languages! ...little by little is fine...

And, we can open up other pathways for communication which are more primal than language. We can learn "body" languages. We can learn shoulder language, forehead language, neck language, hip language, heart language! We can become aware of exactly what is transpiring in our telepathic connections which communicate at lightning speeds. Doing these things, as we shall see, is possible. And they are made very easy by entering into the realms of music and dance!

If you've already rushed to the travel agent and bought your ticket to somewhere you've always wanted to go and decided to begin studying the language of the folks who live there, I recommend figuring out how to suddenly interject a phrase which means *"Surely you must be joking!"*

In English:	*You gotta be kidding!*
In Turkish:	*Shaka yapayorsunuz!*
In Spanish:	*Me estas enganyando!*
In German:	*Zie shatzen voil!*
In Greek:	*Dhe sovaroloyis!*
In Egyptian Arabic:	*Bitharrag!*

These are refreshingly humorous phrases for use at moments of total confusion.

As we widen our searches to "get to know everyone in the whole world," the delightful surprise is that we discover that most individuals the world over are gentle, peace-loving people. This is so much the case that an interesting thing happens: the more we travel, the more we begin to feel safe and surrounded by loving folks everywhere we are.

Breathe delicately...
Watch lovingly...
Listen well...
The lady washing her clothes in the river:
she knows the secrets you have come to ask...

I paid for a room in a fancy hotel
and found myself surrounded by people who advised:
"Don't go out there into the streets! They will kill you for sure!"

The advice didn't ring true and so I went there!
I found myself surrounded by people rushing up to me:
"Welcome!" they exclaimed.
"Why has no one from your country come to visit us for so long?"

WE SHOULD NEVER BELIEVE IN NOR BE CONVINCED BY THE FEARS OF OTHERS

Our own trust in love and friendship is the only reality. If we worry about all the warnings directed at us, we won't end up going anywhere! And if you do go, your own *fear* will *create* a frightening reality. But your own trust and faith will create a *welcoming* reality. It's as *simple* as that.

Sometimes, in our wanderings, we find people trapped under "low ceilings of fear." The low ceilings prevent them from ever looking over the walls to see and greet each other. Years ago I walked into a bar in Belize. After a few minutes I found myself talking with some of the local men.

"It's a good thing you came in here," they told me, "'cause if you'd gone in that bar across the street, they'd have killed you for sure!"

Unable to restrain my own curiosity, I soon found my way over to the bar across the street. "Welcome!" I was soon told. "It's a good thing you came in here and didn't go into that bar across the street! They'd have killed you for sure!"

Low ceilings of fear develop between neighborhoods on every earthly scale and people just won't peek over the top!

It is impossible to observe something without altering it! It's so easy to inadvertently interfere with the subtle workings of another civilization as we move through it and disrupt that which we were hoping to see! Maintain an attitude of humble respect toward all! As a stranger, you are granted a freedom and immunity to classification according to local social class characteristics. You don't fit into any of them. So don't accidentally create a new negative category for yourself. Allow an opportunity to discover yourself as the compassionate person you've always wanted to be!

We get satisfaction when some communication takes place with others whom we had previously felt to be "different." Now we discover that on a deep level we are the same as them. All we have really done is trust the natural attractions that exist between us and remember that "everyone is always right from their own point of view!"

As I said, the more we travel, the more often we will meet people who hold differing beliefs. Every day we can learn to catch ourselves making another one of our own habitual negative judgments. If we can replace these judgments with an open attitude, an endless variety of compassionate beings is revealed before our eyes! How welcome I feel inside my own being when it has been transformed into an entrance toward infinitely varied avenues of compassion! What a relief to trade in my suspicions for this new multi-colored reality! When my mind parades its endless verbal judgments, I drive these judgments into the background and make room for a new reality: everyone is always right from their own point of view! And everyone has compassion to share in ways that I can learn from. This gives me a whole new world of places to address my own empathy!

Once we begin exploring the world, learning its languages and its music and arts, we dive into the fun and gradually lose our fears!

Do We Speak Language
or Does Language Speak Us?

Outside of our window in Cairo the streets are being filled again by men with their prayer mats. There is a small but very active mosque on the street corner. Many times during this lunar month of Ramadan the block has been filled with hundreds of rickety wooden tables, placed end to end with benches on both sides. We walk past.

"Sit down!" someone invites us. Free meals are being created under a nearby tent. Later, we watch once again as the hour of prayer unfolds and hundreds of Egyptians prostrate themselves over and over again in unison. We don't see this unified dance of prayer in America. They are praying. But what, exactly, are they doing? What are they saying? What are they thinking? What are they feeling? What are they accomplishing, if anything? Ah, the mystery...

Whatever is going through their minds is in Arabic. It's going to take us a long journey to fathom what the meaning of this common scene in the Arabic-speaking, Islamic world really is. Calling to mind images of Christians praying in churches in America doesn't seem to help. The texture of that seems completely different: rows of standing or kneeling people speaking or mumbling softly or reading responses from books. These Egyptians are doing something like a dance, and we would like to find some words to help us understand what their full-bodied flowing prayer means.

Find some words...? Language is probably the most powerful tool available to us humans. Ironically, it is also a box which imprisons us. And we frequently don't even know that we have been imprisoned. Words and expressions are pre-packaged in our own language and we can feel like we are being feverishly creative or feel like we are grasping new concepts yet all we may be really doing is re-arranging the pile of ideas currently fashionable in our culture and language. "Hot topics" rise and fall like themes in a national soap opera and we may feel like we're on the cutting edge of exploration when it's really the society in which we are immersed which is wagging our tongues.

Say any of the phrases in the following two columns and notice how streams of emotionally charged thoughts course through your mind. This is what is feels like to have language "speaking you!"

Ethnic Cleansing!	Do-gooders!
The Insurgents!	Axis of Evil!
Freedom Fighters!	Liberals!
Terrorism!	Militants!
Rebels!	Proliferation!
Security!	Weapons of Mass Destruction!
Establishment!	Raw Food!
Subversives!	State-sponsored Terrorism!
Evil!	Western Medicine!
Civilisation!	Extremists!
Democracy!	Acupuncture
Fundamentalist!	Barbarian
Hardliners!	Third World
Dictator!	Al Jazeera
Insurance!	Muslim Clerics

Musical creativity is similar. Composers re-arrange the popular chord changes and melody lines of their times and "create" "new" songs. To bring in new possibilities, it helps to listen to some "gypsy music!"

To stretch our word imagery and bring in something new we tune into the 12th century Persian poet, Rumi! These translations can immediately provide a rich platter of word candy.

Translating common expressions from other languages can yield wonderfully new ways to say things: "the children ran down the hill with their tails in their teeth!" That's a common way, in Arabic, to say "the children ran down the hill lickety-split!"

Once we depart our English language box of tools, all kinds of magic begins to happen. The other day I was listening to a friend giving a talk in a bookstore about her latest published work. She mixed phrases about "worshipping the feminine" and doing our "inner work." She tied these more recent popular phrases to some older ones: "animus and anima," and "Aphrodite," and we all felt satisfied that she had created something new and wonderful.

I couldn't help but think that somewhere at that same moment in Cairo, Egypt there must be an author in a bookstore speaking in Arabic about his or her latest publication. And in Bejing, China there must be another author in another bookstore speaking in Chinese about his or her latest publication. And, in similar fashion, they would be linking currently popular words and phrases to older tried-and-true phrases expressing ancient wisdom in that language which is meaningful to people in that culture, and the audience would be nodding and grinning with excitement and agreement. But, I suspected, there could be a wide gulf between what's popular to talk and think about in new-age America from what's popular to talk and think about in new-age Egypt or China...

Many Americans would wonder: "do they even have popular new-age thinking going on in those cultures?" Well, of course they do. And it's also true that we don't know a thing about it! ...not unless we've learned one of those languages well enough to go and listen to one of those talks and buy and read the books in their original languages. Reading translations can provide a second best way to stay abreast of what's current in another culture but, hey, the likelihood that very many books will actually be translated is small. And then, of course, we wonder about the translation: how much will be lost?

As I continued to listen to my friend describing her book in English, my mind played a strange trick: I began to see the phrases and words coming out of her mouth as little colored geometric shapes. She was producing a torrent of little red triangles, some blue squares, some green spheres, and artfully arranging them into attractive word-paintings! I thought about the Egyptian and Chinese authors over there in their bookstores spouting out little colored geometric shapes in Arabic and Mandarin! I realized that the way we manipulate currently popular thought is by skillfully re-arranging the colors and shapes in our language. It's really very mechanical. Seen in this simplistic way, verbal meaning loses its glamour and we begin to yearn for something deeper; something more universal and closer to whatever it is with which the whole human race vibrates in sacred rhythm. Learning the sacred music and dances from Mongolia would be a good start toward this goal... And, oh yes... sooner or later it will be necessary to actually buy a ticket to Mongolia and sing and dance with the Mongolians!

Those of us born into Indo-European tribes share common patterns of meaning based on the languages we speak while those born into Semitic or Turkish or Chinese or Native American tribes (to mention a few) process meaning in accordance with the grammars and syntactics of their language families. We wonder, "How differently do we think?"

Late night street party in a village beside the Nile River. These Arabic-speaking villagers' ancestors have spoken everything from Pharonic Egyptian, Akkadian and Aramaic, all of the Afro-Asiatic Family, to Greek of the Indo-European Family, and to Turkish, of the Altaic Family.

SOME MAJOR WORLD LANGUAGE FAMILIES

Indo-European Family: (India to Europe to Modern America)
Germanic (German, English, Danish, Dutch, Swedish, Norwegian)
Indo-Iranian (Sanskrit, Hindi, Bengali, Farsi (Persian), Urdu)
Italic or Romance (Spanish, Italian, French, Romanian, Portuguese)
Hellenic (Greek)
Armenian (Western Armenian, Eastern Armenian)
Balto-Slavic (Russian, Polish, Czech, Lithuanian)
Albanian (Gheg, Tosk)
Celtic (Irish and Scottish Gaelic, Welsh)
Anatolian (extinct) (Hittite)
Tocharian (extinct) (Tocharian A, Tocharian B)

Afro-Asiatic Family: (North Africa and the Middle East)
Semitic: (Arabic, Hebrew, Aramaic, Amharic, Tigrinya, Assyrian)
Extinct Semitic: (Akkadian, Phoenician, Ugaritic, Punic, Nabatean, Amorite, Moabite, Syriac)
Berber: (Tuareg, Kabyle)
Cushitic Branch (Somali, Galla, Beja, Afar)
Chadic Branch: (Hausa and 600 other languages in Nigeria)
Egyptian Branch: (extinct) (Ancient Egyptian, Coptic (Orthodox liturgy excepted))

Sino-Tibetan Family: (South-East Asia)
Mandarin, Burmese, Tibetan, and all of the Chinese "dialects"

Uralic Family: (Europe)
Finnish, Estonian and Hungarian

Altaic Family: (Central Asia)
Turkish, Korean, Japanese, Mongol

Caucasian Family: (Western Asia)
Over 40 different languages such as Georgian, Megrelian, Chechen, Ingush Avarian, Lezgian and Dargin

Niger-Kordofanian Family: (Africa)
Over 900 African languages including the subgroups Bantu and Kwa, as well as individual languages such as Swahili, Kikuyu, and Zulu

Austronesian Family: (Polynesian and Indonesian Islands)
Over 900 languages including Hawaiian, Maori, Tagalog, and Malay

Amerindian Family: (North, Central and South America)
Hundreds of Native New World Languages such as Nahuatl, Mayan and Quechua. Many nearing extinction.

The six most commonly spoken languages in the world:
Mandarin Chinese: 950 million speakers (Sino-Tibetan Family: Chinese)
English: 470 million speakers (Indo-European Family: Germanic)
Hindi: 418 million speakers (Indo-European Family: Indo-Iranian)
Spanish: 381 million speakers (Indo-European Family: Romance)
Russian: 288 million speakers (Indo-European Family: Slavic)
Arabic: 219 million speakers (Afro-Asiatic Family: Semitic)

By the time we are two years old, we have already absorbed the way our mother and father's language organizes meaning. And we remain contained in that world view until we make the effort to learn something of a language from a different tribe. If we are English-speaking members of the Indo-European tribe, we must, for example, begin to study something really different: perhaps one of the over 900 Niger-Kordofanian languages from Africa. And we must get to know some of the people who were born into families speaking this language. Some of the thousands of years of the wisdom of their civilization will rub off on you and your personal soul growth will take quantum leaps. Our first language has carved our brain, as it were, into a sculpture of a particular shape. We have become a radio transmitter capable of sending and receiving messages according to certain patterns which we recognize. Our antennae filter out unknown languages and we receive nothing but gibberish from those realms. We forget that whole civilizations are living and breathing in accordance with neural sculptures built from those different shapes. It is possible, as we explore other civilizations, to begin to understand some basically different ways of living human life. It is my belief that there is no real substitute for this. Personal creativity, alas, cannot easily carry you so far.

Bursting into the blazing bright sunlight of new discoveries,
our breath leaves our lungs with the sound of a great wing-stroke!
Amazed, we sit on a brand-new moon and struggle to recover from our dizzy
vertigo!
We look back at the endless tiny circles in which we had been plodding...
We had thought we could find the keys inside those little neighborhoods...
Thank God we bought a ticket and began wandering these ancient spice
markets!

Just how differently we may be thinking is perhaps the most interesting question linguists have tried to explore. Let's look at some ideas about these different ways. A linguist, Benjamin Lee Whorf, maintained that, if Einstein had been born a Hopi Indian and spoken their language, he would have found it easier to express his ideas about relativity. Others, myself included, have looked at the linguistic data supporting his claims and felt that he was making too many assumptions. But his claim has served to spark a lot of open inquiry into the magic of Hopi ways! Frequently we can sense a peoples' magic, but we have difficulty putting our fingers on it! Linguists diving into the music and poetry of a culture have a chance to find something, however: a few clues perhaps!

Loving energy flows easily in Egypt when you take the time to learn a few popular Egyptian love songs.

Arabs, Tibetans, Americans, Chinese...
Islam, Buddhism, Christianity, Judaism, Taoism, Hinduism, Etc...

So Much for the Basics! Let's Explore!

Here are some revelations about Arabic ways of thinking. Arabic is currently the most widely spoken Semitic language. In fact, Arabic is, depending on which statistics you read, either the sixth, fifth or fourth most commonly spoken language in the world today.

Although in American English "Semitic" usually refers to Jews and the Hebrew language, they actually only represent about 1% of the world's current Semitic-language-speaking populations. Hebrew died out as a household lnaguage about 300 years before the time of Christ and survived for centuries only as a liturgical language. Other Semitic languages, notably Aramaic and then Arabic, became the household languages of the Middle East until Hebrew was revived in 1948 with the creation of Israel. Linguists point out, however, that after so many centuries of dis-use, Hebrew needed infusions of modern vocabulary (largely from the Indo-European languages to which the Ashkenazi Jews of Europe had become accustomed) in order to again become a viable household language. Because of this recent somewhat Indo-Europeanized resurrection of Hebrew, some linguists have found that modern Hebrew may no longer share the same underlying structures which characterize other Semitic languages like Arabic and Amharic which have continually evolved in widespread use. Therefore, some of the following theories about the nature of "Semitic thinking" may not entirely apply to speakers of modern Hebrew.

ENGLISH SPEAKERS ARE NOUNS;
ARABIC SPEAKERS ARE VERBS!

Primary meaning in the Arabic language rises out of its verbs. The words for "book," "library," "office," "secretary," "religious scholar," are all built from the Arabic verb "to write." That observation, although not astoundingly significant in itself, gives us a clue about some very basic differences in the ways Arabic speakers process meaning.

"Islam," for example, is not a *noun* in Arabic. It is not the *name* of a religion, but it is a *verb* which describes the act of "submitting" to the will of God. Semitic languages are rooted in "doing" things.

Indo-European languages love to "define" things and make abstract concepts so that it is possible "have" them. Semitic languages are not as good at materialism. When Greeks, who are Indo-Europeans, arrived into the Semitic "holy land" twenty-five hundred years ago they brought high-ranking nouns and sought to package the actions described in the Old Testament, which had never before been committed to writing, into abstract concepts. The evolution of Christianity could be thought of as a process of Indo-Europeanizing and "nominalizing" a Semitic spirituality which originally had meaning in the "doing." Christ would have spoken Aramaic, a Semitic language. But Christianity only became a popular state-sponsored religion three centuries later in the Indo-European world of the Roman Empire! And the Old Testament also had only appeared in written form in Hebrew as a translation back into a Semitic tongue from the Indo-European Greek. So two of the three Abrahamic faiths were first preserved in Indo-European form! Only the third one, Islam, with the committment of the Koran to writing, was actually first preserved in one of the Semitic language of its founders: Arabic.

America to the Arab World: "You must understand:
'freedom,' 'democracy,' 'family values,' 'equal opportunities!'
Why don't you embrace these labels?"

Arab to America: "I see you talk the talk, but do you really walk the talk?"

Our Egyptian friends, praying outside the small mosque on the streets of Cairo, are busy *doing* something: they are actually submitting to the will of God as they prostrate themselves over and over again. I watch with my English-speaking, Indo-European eyes and I try and find an abstraction to fill the "what" of the question "what are they doing?" And I may be missing the point!

Perhaps these Semites, and yes, the ancient Egyptian language was also

Semitic, are not going to be able to answer any questions about "what" they are doing because, in their structure of meaning, that doesn't come up. What means something to them is the "doing" of actually submitting, physically and mentally to the will of God. They will continue to do this five times a day for the rest of their lives and neither be ahead nor behind. To be "ahead or behind" or measure "accumulated prayer energy" you have to *materialize* it first! You have to make it into *something!*

Now that would be a natural approach for an Indo-European, but not for Arabs. What is it that gives the Arab World its legendary mystical magic? Perhaps it's because their way of *"being"* is a *"verb."* Indo-Europeans sometimes seem energetically pale beside the vibrancy of Arab-speaking women and men. The Indo-European way of *"being"* is a *"noun."* The spirituality of the East is frequently associated with exactly this: the *"art of being."*

Why have Buddhism and Hinduism been so much more successfully packaged for understanding by Americans than has Islam? Perhaps it is because both Buddhism and Hinduism grew up in Indo-European, Sanskrit, environments!

It's Christmas! Look under the tree!
My child unwraps the beautiful packages.
Hinduism: in a book!
Buddhism: in another book!
Islam: inside the wrapper we look, but the book has vanished into a perfumed smoke!

My Iraqi friends tell me tales of their upbringing in a country still warm and wholesome before being finally ripped apart by the struggles for control of wealth.

"The way our mother and father managed the energies of their attractions for each other created a sort of household warmth for us children to grow up in which I haven't seen in the West. Imagine your mother and father always, always, always being in a state of loving desire for each other..."

My Iraqi friend was describing an ancient Iraqi unwritten tradition of "Tantric Sexuality," wherein the energy of orgasm is spread carefully through all of life. And of course it is the "unwritten tradition" which most readily makes itself available for us here in the present moment where we actually live. Written traditions are nailed, barely still alive, to the pages and may need to be "interpreted" before becoming useful again.

Could it be that the Semitic Arab World is actually preserving some to the most beautiful ancient ways of "being?" They deserve the utmost honor and protection for their ancient ways and we may have some amazing things to learn from them!

Taoism, growing out of Chinese culture, coincidentally similar to Indo-European languages in its fascination with nouns, has a way of attaching importance to "things."

The Japanese language, however, also purely coincidentally, is similar to Arabic in just this one way: it causes meaning in life to be created by demanding personal manifestation of "verbs." Perhaps what we attribute to "severity" in Japanese Zen practices is actually a manifestation of their focus on repetitively "doing" their prayers. And there is no easy way to "explain" what is being done in neat little word packages. Verbal explanations are sparse in Japanese Zen teachings. Teaching by example is the valued path. But for Indo-Europeans, neat little word packages summarize multiple layers of abstraction which can then be tucked away on the bookshelf like so many carbohydrate meals for the winter.

Perhaps the particular vibrancy of the Semitic World could be seen as akin to the vibrancy of a pre-agricultural society. Nuts and seeds and meat are filled with healthy, energy-giving fats which cannot be stored for long periods without going rancid. Hunter-gatherer peoples evolved into couch potatoes only after an agricultural revolution (about seven or eight thousand years ago) which allowed the storage of sugars, in their various carbohydrate forms, to be shelved, as I say, for the winter! Then they could settle down to some well-deserved laziness and get sleepy.

As we learned to store ideas in abstract nouns we realized that we could also put them on the shelves "for the winter." We could *"have"* ideas that way. And we could *"have"* religion that way too! Two of the surviving modern religions, Judaism and Christianity, both owe their roots to Semitic peoples. But as we have seen, Semites throughout early history were so busy *"being"* their religions that, as we have seen, it wasn't until Indo-European Greek-speakers put those religions "on the shelf for the winter" by writing them down that they became something more than series of tales handed down by word of mouth!

Sufism is the "esoteric" brand which seeks to return to the *"being"* roots of Islam. The non-Semitic cultures in both Turkish and Persian regions have adopted Islam and frequently formulate traditions which they label as "Sufi." I have found, not surprisingly, a general reluctance in the Arab world where Semitic spontaneity is still highly venerated to advertise "Sufi" groups. In the words of Hamza el Din, a well-known oud-playing musician from southern Egypt: "Anyone who says that they are a Sufi is not a Sufi."

As money was invented, we could *"have"* stored human energy on the shelf as well. After all, for "sixty dollars" one can hire another man to dig a ditch. The guy with the money is the guy who is best with "nouns." He's the guy who likes to organize the action. The guy who is best with the "verbs" is the one who ends up out there digging the ditch. He likes to do the action. (You can understand your daughter's attraction to him but you wouldn't want her to end up marrying him if you want her to be rich.) But it's also the guy who becomes the verbs who needs to go see the doctor less. His is the more physically healthy lifestyle (as long as social forces and alcohol don't drag him down.) So it has become advisable for the guys who are good with the nouns to go to the gym and try and "stay in shape." And somewhere deep in the Indo-European noun-loving soul is an ancient hunger for *doing* and for the art of *"being-with-great-intensity."* Hence the magic, for Westerners, of the ancient East...

INDO-EUROPEAN MATERIALISM

It's interesting that in Arabic there is no active way to "have" something. There is no common verb translatable as "to have." Things are "to you" or "for you" or "with you"... always attached loosely in this prepositional way... There are kingly verbs to describe formal ownership, but they are not used in common street language. Is this why many traditional Arabs are less materialistic than Indo-Europeans?

While acknowledging that poverty creates desperate material needs in any people, it has been noticed since ancient times that the traditions of hospitality run deep in the Arab World, so deep in fact, that battles have been lost at moments when it was impossible to fight an enemy because some of its members were guests in an Arab household! The British watched in dismay early in the twentieth century as Arab armies refused to advance to drive out the Ottoman armies because they had Turkish guests in their homes at that moment. There were times when the tactical advantage was lost because of their insistence on honoring this ancient tradition.

Hospitality in the Arab World does not, however, offer "the honor of submitting to God" to non-believers. An anthropologist from India[1] who wanted to join in prayer with villagers from the Nile Delta was discouraged apparently for not being "qualified" to "be" with them at that moment. And there have been times when worshipping Muslims have been made to feel like biological specimens by interested Westerners, a mutually uncomfortable relationship.

MATERIALIZING RELIGION

Western European and American scholars have examined the world's "great religions" as if they were entities separate from the people who live within them. This yields very interesting "scientific information." But, just as science has had difficulty with descriptions of paranormal "psychic" realities because they are subject to still invisible laws which make them horrendously unpredictable, scientific study of great religions has had limited success. It's a bit like trying to describe what it feels like to breathe water if you are not a fish.

As these European scholars studied and objectified religion, which "once referred to acting piously, it became known instead as an identity. Religion changed from something you *did* into something that you *were*. Instead of you owning your religion (as an act that you do) and being responsible for your religion (your acts of religiosity), you instead belonged to your religion; it became something that owns you. A whole complex of subtle psychological shifts takes place between people and religion: by the end of this shift, Religion, Inc. owns people, and religion becomes responsible for people instead of the other way around. Such is the power of language over how we think and therefore how we act."[2]

THE ART OF SPIRITUAL SURRENDER

In Arabic, it's virtually impossible to say something in the future tense without the concomitant expression: "insha'Allah." "Insha'Allah" means "God willing." An interesting way of being seems to derive from this divorcing of future events from human will. If you have agreed to meet your friend the next day and he doesn't show up you don't have a category for being upset with him because, after all, it was God's will who controlled whether he showed up or not! When we are in the Arab World we notice that people don't waste their time apologizing for plans gone astray. Everyone already knows that God simply willed something else to happen and no one is to blame! Interestingly, it seems to be very difficult to play the "victim" role in their culture. No one's will is involved other than God's. You're not going to easily become angry with God! This frees your energy up to proceed seamlessly and without whining to Plan B. When you do see your friend who didn't show up and you, because you come from an Indo-European way of thinking, ask him why he was absent, he will probably be very surprised that such a question would even come up. He won't have some story at his fingertips. He'll be caught by surprise that anyone would even ask such a thing and perhaps have difficulty even calling back to mind whatever sequence of events had occurred the day before which changed his fate and led to his not keeping the appointment.

Once your Indo-European mind realizes that, while you're in the Arab world, you might as well not even bother asking such questions, you realize that there's a whole open creative space for moving forward with new ideas which you had customarily clouded with a lot of blame and victim-oriented thinking.

What a breath of fresh air! You are in a culture where serendipity rules! What a relief! If you can learn from this other culture how to let go of attachments to past plans as quickly as the moment becomes "now," then you have learned one of the keys to ultimate human freedom! What a gift! And just think: your first impulse had been to become annoyed! Perhaps you thought you were not being given proper consideration because you were a foreigner. It takes some observing of how Arab World people handle their own "missed appointments" among themselves before all of this can become clear.

HOW TO 'MAKE SOMEONE DO SOMETHING" IN TIBETAN

I once spent a year working in the Linguistics department at the University of California in Berkeley with a Tibetan Lama to learn something of the Tibetan language. One day I asked Lama Kunga how to translate: "I made my son go to the store."

"You cannot say that in Tibetan," was his immediate response. This was strange because he generally found ways to translate things. So the next day I asked him again if he had thought of a way to translate "I made my son go to the store."

"The closest you can come in Tibetan," he responded, "is to say that 'I caused my son to cause himself to go to the store.'"

Well, if you come from a tribe where there is no way to "make somebody do something," except by creating a sympathetic resonance, then just imagine all the possible differences in ways of living! If each person must take personal responsibility for his own actions because the very grammar of the language doesn't describe absolute coercion, then the whole psychology could be very different for people living in Tibet.

BEING A GOOD LISTENER CHINESE STYLE

Some additional interesting examples of ways in which "language speaks us," if we are Chinese, were provided by Dr. Kenneth DeWoskin, Professor of Chinese at the University of Michigan. Remember also, Chinese is in the same language family as Tibetan.

"Wisdom and enlightenment for native speakers of Chinese will most likely come through auditory channels. Listening is more important than seeing. Words in English like 'visionary' or 'seer' would be best translated into Chinese words which literally mean 'listener.' There is a deep reverence for harmony as exemplified by sympathetic resonances. The plucked string on one musical instrument will cause a similarly tuned string on another instrument to cause itself to also resonate. Ancient Chinese ways of seeing order in the universe depend heavily on mutual resonances between realms...

"As Chinese wisdom is exemplified by the art of being a 'good listener,' Chinese spiritual awakening is equated with being able to hear 'the music' played by a master musician on an instrument which has had its strings removed! Sympathetic resonance is occurring inaudibly!

"Some translators of the Chinese word 'kuan', meaning literally, 'tube,' 'pipe,' or 'resonator,' have expanded the meaning to include 'manage' or 'control' as English equivalents."[3]

In other words, a kind of "pied piper" syndrome is implied. A musician skillfully playing on a flute, which is a "tube" or "pipe", can be said to be "managing" or "controlling" his audience.

Coming back to Lama Kunga's revelations concerning Tibetan language, which is, as I said, related to Chinese, we realize that the same principle is being described. We can't "make" our son go to the store, but we can provide a background of harmonious living which will cause him to feel like going to the store for us. Only when there is a sympathetic resonance can communication and cooperation happen!

Just how knowing these things can help one navigate Chinese or Tibetan culture I don't know, but it makes me want to go find out! Awareness of these kinds of ancient wisdom can help us open our senses to hearing the pulsing heart-beats of humanity all over the planet!

REMEMBER WHO IS RELATED TO WHOM

Take another look at the list of languages in the vast Indo-European family. When I say "Indo-European" to describe our English-speaking minds, I am referring to the ways of thinking of a vast collection of tribes who speak languages related to English. We all, in essence, think alike. Our Indo-European tribe, as the name implies, extends from Hindus in northern India all the way to our American English! We are related to the people in Northern India, Pakistan, Afghanistan, Iran, Tadjikistan, Russia, Armenia, Greece, Albania, Germany, Sweden, Norway, Latvia, France, Romania, Italy, Ireland... to name a few...

Many Americans are surprised to learn that we are part of the same tribe as are people in Iran and Afghanistan. The word "Iran" is, also surprisingly to many of us, the same word as "Aryan." Somewhere around the Black Sea close to Iran is thought to be the birthplace of the Indo-European language family some 15,000 years ago. As long as our travels through the world remain in Indo-

European places, ways of life will remain somehow familiar and intelligible to us English speakers.

The moment we move, however, from Indo-European Northern India into the Dravidian cultures of Southern India, or we go from Indo-European Iran into Semitic Iraq, we will be surrounded by mystery. And mystery is uncomfortable for most people until they come to terms with the reality of this and develop another level of faith. When you finally become comfortable with being "lost" 80% of the time, you are a traveler. And it's not until we travel outside of the Indo-European world and experience that degree of separation that we can begin to understand first, how different, and finally, how similar, we all are!

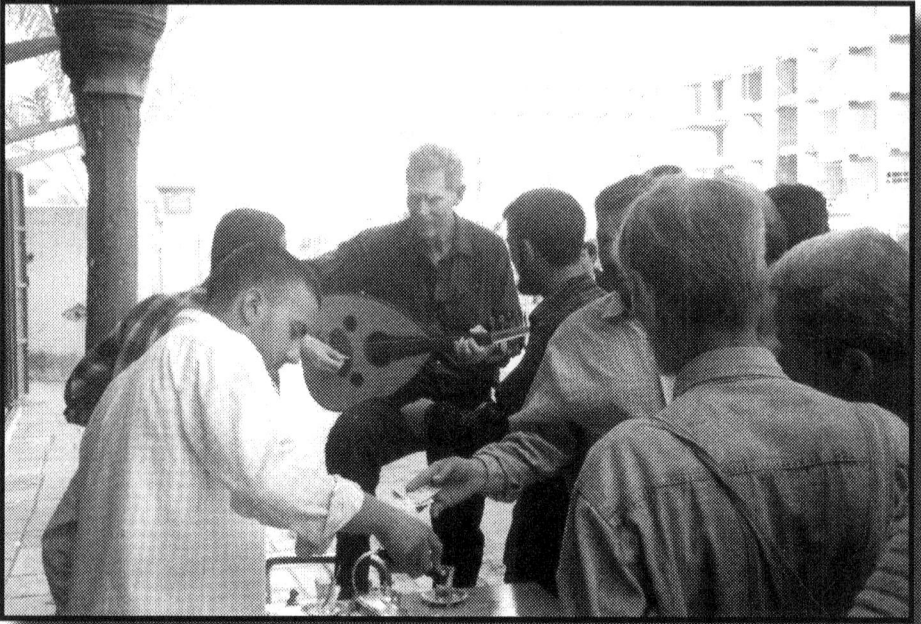

Singing with Iraqi Men in Baghdad, Iraq, in spring of 2003.
The air is filled with smoke from burning buildings.
Their favorite songs are, of course,
in Iraqi Arabic.

Seeing People in the Street

Having discovered the incredible adventure of exploring ways of being in different ancient civilizations, how do we begin? We may meet a Mongol or a Mayan. We sense by looking into his or her eyes that we have different ways of processing things. We know that it's not possible to literally translate these different ways from one language family to another. So we begin to learn the art of telepathic soul absorption. We allow the windows into our soul to open toward this foreign person we have just met and we peer into the windows open into his or her soul. And we find some transmission, some radiation, some energetic exchange is happening.

Here is an exercise which can be done immediately upon landing in a foreign country which will give results. It helps prepare you for communication, verbal and telepathic, with new friends anytime anywhere.

Go and sit somewhere where lots of people are walking by. Let's suppose, for now, that you just landed at the airport in a country where the people and the language are new to you. You have taken a taxi to a hotel and now you have some time to go explore the city. You are sitting somewhere and you are watching the people walking by. They look different than people from your home town. They have different expressions on their faces; they have different postures, different ways of moving their bodies, and, of course, they speak a different language.

a) Focus your attention on someone who is walking down the street.
b) Look at him or her carefully and imagine that you are inside his or her body looking out through his or her eyes.
c) Imagine you are thinking about whatever he or she is thinking about.
d) Imagine that, although this foreigner is thinking in a different language, that you are also thinking in that language.
e) Imagine knowing that your view and interpretation of the world as seen through this new pair of eyes is just as "correct" or "right" as you customarily feel your own ideas to be.
f) Watch the way his or her body moves as he or she walks and pretend you are feeling that same motion from inside his or her body. Feel how it feels to hold your shoulders like that; move your hips like that. Keep pretending that you are the one inside that body of that person you see walking down the street. You are

perhaps on an errand to meet someone you know and arrange some details of business or family. This is just another day in what is to you, because you live nearby, a familiar part of the city.

g) Imagine that you are sharing the consciousness of a well-adjusted compassionate individual, always ready and willing to help others who are in need and share the atmosphere of the loving family and community in which you live.

h) Sooner or later you will have occasion to greet someone who lives in this city. It may be a waiter in a restaurant; it may be the lady who sells postcards in the little shop. When this happens, remember the "seeing people on the street" exercises with which you have prepared yourself for this moment. For an instant you look into each others' eyes and you smile because he or she smiles and he or she smiles because you smile and on some level of faith, you already know each other...

Here are some of the ways this exercise has unfolded for me. The languages used can be a mix of whatever phrases you have gained knowledge of and whatever knowledge of the English language others might have.

You realize your photos are ready to be picked up... the streets are jammed --- it's a Ramadan moon over Cairo... ten o'clock at night.... you begin walking toward the photo shop... someone is beside you – you greet him "Asalaam aleikum..." "wa aleikum assalaam" – effortless and soft connection... you ask him for directions – you walk together... he asks where you are from and you tell him – you are already inside the collective consciousness of the Cairo streets... everything seems easy... he asks if you've seen the pyramids or been to Luxor and you tell him... you ask him if he's from Cairo and what he does for a living... he tells you that he's an accountant who has lived in Cairo for 15 years... you arrive to the photo shop and say "maa'salaameh"... may you go in safety... see ya later... bye... you wave politely at each other and part ways... the next afternoon the same thing happens, only this time it's a fourth-grade schoolgirl, eager to practice her English and help you find your way... you begin to feel more and more at home no matter where you are walking on planet earth... now you are in a village in Peru, now a Palestinian refugee camp in Damascus, Syria... now in Athens, Greece... now you are in Baghdad, in Iraq... now with Iraqi refugees in Amman, Jordan... you learn to sing part of a local popular song... now you are invited to eat and to stay in one of your new friends' houses... you sing parts of the song again... you buy a musical instrument and learn to play part of the same song on the instrument... you carry your instrument down the street and when someone asks you to play it you sit down and play it and sing... you accept invitations... you see these people in their strength, in their hospitality, in their giving... of whatever they have... now you ask yourself what it is that you have that you wish to give to them... you realize it is your heart... this is

36

more important than new technology... you have tasted the hospitality in North America and in the Middle East, the Balkans and Latin America. Linger there. Savor and learn from the different textures...

After some time spent together with your new friends, you take a break... you discover that you can sit in silence on your new friend's couch and rest for a while... it's not necessary to fill all of the time with words or action...

Young Syrian men, appreciative of the fact that we have learned some of their favorite songs in Syrian Arabic, extend us a warm welcome.

Dealing with Fear

Lurking in the corners of our daily decision-making;
Hiding behind our smiles;
Sneaking into our health and into our breath,
The One we all try to deny...

Fear flaps her black wings through the sky once again...

A Syrian friend who made certain that we would be invited to play Arabic music in his favorite local restaurant.

Reflections of Fear

Once we felt a strange twinge in our stomach and it turned out to be the flu. We got sick and we recovered. A few weeks later we felt another strange twinge. Remembering our flu, we feel a rising panic: "Oh no! I am getting sick again!" The panic is causing a torrent of strange unpleasant sensations. "Oh no! Perhaps I am coming down with something even more horrible!"

An hour later, distracted by a visit from a friend, we realize that we feel fine. "What was that all about?" we ask ourselves. We have a slightly uneasy realization that sometimes we can't distinguish a real germ attack from a fear attack!

Can we poison our friendships with our own fear and mistrust?
Can fear actually create attacks?
What happens when a whole society becomes obsessed with fear?
Will demonizing a race of people eventually elicit some demons?

It is certainly true that unfavorable views of the American government are increasingly common outside of America. It is unfortunate, but obviously true, that our fear of terrorism will eventually create more terrorism. Fear-driven people and societies don't make very healthy decisions. If their obsessions with fear and their quests for personal safety cause a paranoia to creep into their ways of relating to others; if people are treated like terrorists for long enough, some of them will become terrorists.

The rest of the world is not a scary place. Even in spite of the legacy of aggression for which the U.S. government has now become famous, we found that, in the 5 months we have spent in Iraq, Syria, Jordan, Egypt and the West Bank since the fall of 2002, we haven't received even one rude comment as a result of our announcing ourselves to be Americans.

Arab World people know that governments don't usually represent people. After all, they haven't had the freedom to create governments of their own for 800 years now. The Arab people I know see all too clearly that their governments have been either been set up by the British, French and Americans in recent times or emerged out of desperate and fundamentalist reaction to those colonialist governments.

Even back in the 13th century, the arrivals of the Mongols, the Portuguese and the Turks prevented the formation of Arab governments representative of the egalitarian spirit that many Arabs see in Islam.

An Arab friend told me decades ago: "What you don't understand is that, for us Arabs, there is no 'Saudi Arabia!'"

Until the arrival of British domination, the Middle East was still a land where "nations" were defined by tribes who spoke the same language. If the people moved, the "nation" moved. Fuzzy borders could self-correct relatively easily and involved less violence. Given the evolution of modern map-making and our relatively new-found ability to draw lines to carve up what's left of the earthly pie in the face of burgeoning populations, we can only wish that someone other than the British had decided where to draw those lines. Local folks surely would have been able to do a better job. The lines around Saudi Arabia, Jordan, Syria, Lebanon, Iraq, and, of course, Israel, have all been drawn by foreigners.

So when American citizens show up, as we do in the Arab world, as long as we're not wearing uniforms, we will be sympathetically viewed as fellow citizens of the world who, like themselves, are having to live under the rule of strange governments who follow nonsensical rhythms and patterns.

Ask any cab driver in the Arab world. He'll throw up his hands and express powerlessness and confusion when it comes to comprehending governments. "All we can do is live our lives as best as we can in these difficult situations!"

Overcoming Fear: Check out the Statistics! You may be SAFER over there!

Whenever Kristina and I return from our travels in the Arab World, people here in America immediately comment, "Thank God you're back and you're safe!"

We appreciate the concern for our well-being. But what our fellow Americans generally don't know is that we're actually probably safer in the Arab World than we are here in America. Their society seems less violent and more crime-free.

Let's begin by taking a look at the number of American civilian citizens killed by "terrorist" attacks since 9/11. In 2002, according to the US State Department, 27 American citizens were killed world-wide in "terrorist" attacks. The number rose to 35 in 2003. The State Department's definition of "terrorist attack" is as follows: "premeditated, politically motivated violence perpetrated against noncombatant targets by sub-national groups or clandestine agents, usually intended to influence an audience."

According to the US State Department:
2002 – Total US citizens killed on planet earth as result of terrorist attack: 27
2003 – Total US citizens killed on planet earth as result of terrorist attack: 35
This is 0.01 American people per 100,000 per year (1 person in 10 million per year)

We can compare these numbers with:

2002 – Total US citizens killed inside America by adverse reactions to legally prescribed drugs: 84,000
This is 28 per 100,000 per year (2800 people in 10 million)

2002 – Total US citizens killed inside America by traffic accidents: 33,000
This is 11 per 100,000 per year (1100 people in 10 million)

Typing "international crime statistics" into an internet search engine and following some of the thousands of resulting threads yields some interesting facts.

Deaths from random criminal violence averaged over the last 10 years, for example:

Estonia (one of most dangerous countries): 30 people per 100,000 per year

Egypt (one of safest countries): 1 person per 100,000 per year

USA (medium danger): 8 people per 100,000 per year

Israel/Palestine (medium danger): 14 people per 100,000 per year

Mexico (medium danger): 19 people per 100,000 per year

Generally, statistics in the Arab-speaking countries regarding numbers of people who die from random violence are ranging from 1 to 5 people per 100,000 per year. That is, as we can see, somewhat lower than statistics for America. In Israel/Palestine, as we can also see, the statistics are higher, but not as high as in Estonia or Mexico. And many would consider Israel/Palestine to be a war zone. And statistics for Israel/Palestine may be getting worse.

It may be that non-lethal crimes such as theft, domestic abuse and rape are considerably less common in the Arab World than in either Europe or North or South America. Reliable statistics on some of these crimes are hard to find. Peoples' impressions differ. My impression is that theft happens much less in Arab countries because the tightly knit, clan-oriented fabric of their societies doesn't permit maverick behavior. But at the same time, Arabs from Jordan and Syria, for example, believe that theft rates are higher in Egypt than in their own countries and express fearing theft when they travel there. An American calculated that being at home in Kansas City was 97 times more dangerous than being in Sanaa, the capital of Yemen. Depending on where you are coming from and what you are used to will determine your attitudes towards danger. Most people don't ever bother to really look at world-wide statistics to calculate realistic relative risks. And government-issued "travel-advisories" don't seem to either.

Domestic violence and rape are always hard to measure anywhere in the world. It's hard to find statistics since it is basically a taboo subject.

I have heard of a Western woman being raped in a tourist area hotel. And I have heard Western women complain about being the victims of unwanted advances. No society condones the violence of rape. I have known enough American and European women, however, who have traveled Mediterranean countries actually hoping for cross-cultural sexual adventures, that I can see how local men, especially around tourist areas where alcohol flows, can be led to anticipate the possibility of meeting these mysterious and "loose" women. They would seldom expect such behavior from women from their own cultures, as the fabric of tribal and family connections defines romantic availability in very strict terms.

We have all, of course, heard of prisoners, both female and male, being raped by members of police or military organizations controlled by the super-wealthy and the super-powerful.

But the ordinary Arab-speaking friends we have claim that they have rarely ever heard of this happening amongst themselves. Of course we can never know the extent to which such events may be hidden, but our female Arab World friends seem to universally claim to feel safe on the streets any time night or day.

People can be locked into family structures that are not of their choosing. "Marital rape" is a term which has been created to describe this. Still, the vast majority of Arab-speaking friends we have met seem to have deeply loving partnerships. The atmosphere of love feels very rich between husbands and wives and their children.

So really, when people in America so commonly greet us with comments such as "Thank God you're back and you're safe!" it's clear that the spreading of fear has created a distortion of the facts.

According to Interpol, the international agency within which police from different countries communicate and cooperate, it is true that violent crimes exist in every country in the world. Most people would rather believe that "it's somewhere else" that the really dangerous people live. That's why we must look at statistics to balance our perceptions about safety, danger and crime.

Summary information from a Special United Nations Global Report:
Arab states generally reported very low rates for nearly all types of crime.
Theft rates were higher for industrial countries than non-industrial countries.
High homicide rates were reported for several Latin American cities, New York and Northern European cities.

Statistics from FBI summaries regarding USA violent crime rates in 2002:
Murder: 5.6 people per 100,000 per year national average
(With hot spots such as Washington DC: 50 people per 100,000 per year)
Murder during Rape: 0.04 people per 100,000 per year
Rape: 58 people per 100,000 per year
Severe Abuse by Spouse or Partner: 2105 people per 100,000 per year
Alcohol is involved in 30% of violent crimes between strangers and 75% of violent crimes between intimates.
This is interesting when we compare USA violence against Islamic world violence. Since alcohol is seldom consumed (except by the wealthiest

Westernized class) in the Islamic world, it cannot be a factor in violence. Our experience has been that, except in tourist parts of Cairo where alcohol is consumed, the absence of alcohol from the social and musical events we have attended or created has made it very clear that gentleness and respect prevail as gatherings progress late into the night.

The collection and availability of statistics on violence is uncertain and incomplete in every country in the world, but here are some statistics on violence from two Arab-language countries:

Egypt:
Murder: 1.26 per 100,000 per year
Honor killings of women: 0.08 per 100,000 per year

Jordan:
Murder: 2.5 people per 100,000 per year
Honor killings of women: 0.6 women per 100,000 per year

The Arab world has low crime rates in general, but women there are also still commonly regarded as property and ancient pre-Islamic tribal honor codes can lead to "honor killings" of women. "Nobody can really want to kill his wife or daughter or sister," said Mohammed Ajjarmeh, chief judge of the High Criminal Court in Jordan. "But sometimes circumstances force him to do this. Sometimes, it's society that forces him to do this, because the people won't forget. Sometimes, there are two victims – the murdered and the murderer."

In countries where strict *Islamic* justice codes are the law, these honor killings are much less frequent. People there don't feel as though they have to take the law "into their own hands." It is more in countries where European colonial powers installed the governments that the problem persists. The Koran specifies that "the testimony of four male witnesses" is required as conclusive evidence of sexual misconduct and this virtually never is even possible. "Treat your women well, and be kind to them," the Prophet Mohammed is recorded as saying.

In other words, it is primarily when ancient *pre-Islamic* tribal honor codes are prevailing, which date back to times long before Mohammed walked the earth, that these "honor killings" occur. They apparently occur less often in places where Islamic judges are empowered.

Women are still apparently treated to some degree as "property" in many societies.

In August of 2004, the Catholic Pope's Congregation for the Doctrine of the Faith (known as "The Inquisition" back in the glory days) released a "major statement" on the status of women. They declared that women who resist their subordination to men too strongly are "giving rise to harmful confusion" and perverting their "natural characteristics" of "listening, welcoming, humility, faithfulness, praise and waiting."

Thailand has become known for its trafficking of child "sex slaves" as well as adult "sex workers."

The trafficking of female "sex slaves," especially of Russian origin, is rampant in Israel. "Women trafficked from Eastern Europe, are stripped and sold naked as slaves to Tel Aviv traders for US$500-1,000. Smuggling, fraudulent documents, collaboration between police and brothel owners are involved. There are routine brutal beatings and sexual abuse. There are over 10,000 women in prostitution in Tel Aviv. Men pay for 25,000 acts of prostitution there every day."[4]

Saudi Arabian family members, both male and female, have been known to abuse (sexually and otherwise) the Indonesian and Sri Lankan women who work in their households as servants. The extreme imbalance of wealth between the oil-rich kingdom and the impoverished population from further east contributes to the prevalence of this abuse. The fundamentalist nature of Saudi Wahabi Islam may also give fewer options for Saudi citizens to be sexually expressive and this, as we know, causes pressures to build up.

Visiting Westerners are seldom in positions to be threatened by either the prostitution in Tel Aviv or the oppression of Asians in Saudi Arabia.

THE HUMAN NORM:
DEIFY, DON'T DEMONIZE, OUR SEX DRIVE

Men and women alike feel outrage at violence against women wherever it occurs. I wonder to what extent the outrage felt by men is an extension of their patriarchal sense that, as "owners of women," it is their duty to "protect" them. And this "protection" ends up further inhibiting women's freedom.

The male sex drive is frequently very powerful and fuels violence against others and against selves in very complex ways.

Fortunately, I believe that the vast majority of peoples on earth have found ways to honor this most ancient aspect of life. Obviously, our sexual energies are not going to disappear. Deification of our sex drives results in channeling this energy into beautiful family relations and beautiful creativity.

Hosome "spiritual" teachings demonize this powerful sex drive along with other "evils."
Here is a quote from a conservative Naqshabandi Sufi doctrine:

"Have you seen those who make their Desires their LORD?
Drinking, smoking, drugs, fornication, anger and many other vices.
These are all **Lords** over you.
That is why many people cannot stop committing evil.
That wickedness is very powerful and has a tremendous hold over people."

We can find similar anti-sex codes in "spiritual" teachings from many parts of the world. Although there may be men on these paths who are channeling their sex drive in healthy ways, it is also possible that repression of the male sex drive can result in other unpredictable types of violence.

FEAR OR EXCITEMENT:
A QUICK LEAP CALLED COURAGE

Even though we have now studied enough statistics to intellectually realize that there are no great dangers out there in the world and that we are basically free to wander where we will, there may be times when we feel adrenaline pumping through our bodies as we enter unfamiliar territories.
At those times we can use our minds to label the sensation "excitement!" rather than "fear." This will help you be able to move forward creatively into the new situation rather than run backwards and away from it.

OhmiGod! I'm feeling really really... EXCITED!
(Don't use the 'F' word 'frightened' or the 'S' word 'scared'!)

Why courage?
The penalties for a fear-driven life-style reverberate through the atmosphere bringing disease, or at least "dis-ease," to all involved.
We need to cultivate our courage to help us make healthy choices, not little by little as the years go by, but by leaps and bounds at this very moment!

Fear of Learning Languages

"What if I make a mistake? I wouldn't dare open my mouth!" With fears like this it's not easy to practice new tongues in foreign places.

Americans have felt that their culture has been the focus of world attention for the last century. The whole world, it seems, is learning English. So why bother, we ask ourselves, learning other languages. Life in America has become so circumscribed, so cross-culturally unadventurous, that people have become afraid of interactions in any way unfamiliar. The sad truth is that an immeasurable variety of human culture is being lost as the world learns English.

On the bus in Mexico: the child's eyes look into mine with such a power of pure
clean love that my soul has been uplifted for all of eternity... hello...
In Central Egypt: every farmer bending over those crops beside the Nile has a
secret for me to learn... if only...
In the back of a Peruvian truck: a young Inca boy with dancing energy eyes...
How do I find out...
In the Greek tavern on the southern shore of Crete:
the old man dances and gazes out over the Mediterranean... I want to know...
Turkish village: alone with this lovely maiden in the family garden...
The powerful perfume of sacred flirtation... wait... how...
Egyptian village: women and children cuddle up to me in their mud house...
chickens and pigs wander through the kitchen... we snuggle and we sing...

To drink from the many flavored wines of human languages we must travel and we must learn *how to learn* these languages. For anyone who has reached the point of uttering even short phrases in a "foreign" language it has been a delightful shock to discover how enriching and empowering that feels! Ecstatic, you realize how much you have just grown! This "foreign language" is suddenly not entirely foreign any more. It doesn't matter that your skill isn't even up to that of the average local 3-year-old native speaker. You are spontaneously communicating in this new language and you are beginning to form thoughts in your mind in this new language.

Returning back home to America you are confronted with wall to wall comments: "I am no good at learning languages!" you hear over and over again from your friends.

What a shame! America is a country wherein people have created a mythology about how impossible it is to learn languages! "If you don't learn as a child, it's not possible to learn," goes one such myth. Well if that's true, how come my Tunisian friend, who arrived two years ago in Florida unable to even tell a taxi driver whether to go "right" or "left" in English was able to deliver an eloquent 15 minute speech in English in front of a TV camera less than two years later? If he can learn a new language in 2 years, why can't we? The truth is that we adults have tools for learning with which we can run circles around children. If we decide to do it, we can learn a new language much faster than a child can. The child might be able to imitate pronunciation details and slang expressions more easily if he's surrounded by children on a playground, but when it comes to actually learning words and structures of speech, adults can proceed a dozen times more rapidly.

"But I could never become 'fluent,'" another friend says. Well, that's true. Few non-native speakers will ever become as fluent as someone born and raised in the culture. But just because you might have an accent and some limitations does not mean you shouldn't proceed. Just because you may not perform on stage does not mean that you should never sing!

Spend $30 on a book and a CD or tape and see how far you can get! You have nothing to lose and so much to gain. Anyone busy with learning a new language can tell you that there is no "right way" to learn. Buy language programs, dictionaries, take classes, learn popular songs, practice with native speakers who live in your town. Be persistent. Read your study materials during lunch. Listen to the tapes as you drive your car. The day will come when a little baby soul will be born inside you while you are traveling in that "foreign" country. That country will then no longer be "foreign" to you. You will have become part of the social fabric.

It is, of course, possible, to live in an American community in a foreign country and still never learn to speak the local language. If you end up in such a community, make a strong effort right from the start to escape its confines. If you don't, you run the risk of creating habit patterns around *not* learning. There will always be plenty of Americans there who will perpetuate the myths about, not only the supposed impossibility of learning, but about some supposed distasteful qualities of the local population. Don't allow yourself to get trapped. Learn to say "tomato" in the local language today, read my poem entitled "tomatoes" at the end of this book and go out into the market place to buy one!

Feeling Good

Your flower petals are open to receive the sunshine.
Your limbs are already dancing to a smooth cadence.
Your juices are flowing and you feel well-oiled inside.
Who is stronger: your rider or your horse?

This Egyptian woman must rise to dance to this music.

Sensuality and Music
You Have to Feel Good Inside

Making small movements with our wrists, we give our energy to the world! A dozen smiling faces look skyward and graciously acknowledge the gift. What is this magic? I don't know, but it happens easily when we dance.

Some days we just don't have it. Our best efforts fall short. We sing a song of love but it just doesn't carry. We hatch a plan to help humanity, send it out into the streets and... No one notices. What happened?

I guess we just have to acknowledge that some days we're on and some days we're not. We've all noticed this.

What is it that gives wings to our intentions?

We have to feel the energy flowing inside before it can become visible outside. And only *you* can discover what it is that makes your own energy flow. Others may have a thousand suggestions, a thousand pieces of advice, but only *you* will know when you have discovered the secret. What are the things that make you feel really good inside? Is it being on your cross-country skis in the white wintry wilderness? Is it going to your yoga or aerobics class? Is it dancing? Is it meditating? Is it playing music for others to dance? Is it backpacking through the green forest? Is it drawing or painting?

Are we spending the time we need to spend cultivating our own energies?

If not, why not? Are we blocking something? Let's try and look...

This Egyptian man is also feeling good and must also rise to dance.
We think that this is nothing, but it is more than that: it is magic.

Sacred Flirtation

"Sacred Flirtation" is the basic energy of attraction which exists between all people. We all have the right to stay connected with other people by allowing the ethereal energies of attraction to connect us. I experience very outgoing flirtation in the Arab World cultures. The attraction between men and women is very obvious. The attraction between men and men is very open. I'm not talking about creating sexual liaisons. I'm simply talking about "energetically dancing" together, sometimes externally and sometimes internally. And the attractions between women and women are also clearly visible.

Drawn to the entertainment districts of tropical towns... we wander, young and brimming with energy... the open air dance clubs are part of the human garden... Learning... learning... learning... we find the sweet spots where the dance and the flirtation flow with a musical harmony... live musicians play in every courtyard... we dance... we flirt... sometimes we make love in a rented room... mostly, we bathe in the thick perfume of attractions... we walk the streets and learn to navigate that thick perfume... finally, we choose to keep the perfume in our nostrils... we dance... we flirt... we breathe... we dance... we flirt... sometimes we touch...

Musicians and dancers live in a thick and busy atmosphere of sacred flirtation. Jealousies arise around us. Many people don't understand what we are doing, but are still attracted. They may try to own us. That doesn't work.

Those who understand what we are doing, keeping the air safe for sacred flirtation, honor us and we know that we must continue to bathe in this perfume. We remain healthy and washed clean of stagnant energies.

Belly dance is one of the world's most sensual and feminine styles. It makes people feel good to be in the presence of a dancer who is comfortable with her sensuality. There are limits on how much of this energy women and men can exchange outside of a marriage or love relationship.

This is true in both the East and the West. In the East, the attraction between the sexes is considered to be so strong that it is best not to get close to letting it out except in privacy. They suggest walking around with beauty somewhat under cover in public. This is true for both women and men. In the West many people try to deny that the strength of this attraction exists in such powerful ways. Women may wear bikinis to the beach and then be caught in the uncomfortable position of simultaneously wanting to be seen and not wanting to be seen. Men can similarly be caught in the uncomfortable position of wanting both to look and to flirt and having to pretend that nothing is happening.

Now a belly dancer, with her warm, mature and sensual moves can become a moving magnetic bridge which allows women and men to breathe into the reality of our powerful attractions for one another. At Arab-world weddings this dance is a time-honored sacred aspect of the ceremony and is enjoyed by men, women and children alike. For every movement made in public by the dancer, there have been thousands of sensual movements made among grandmothers and grand-daughters and mothers and sisters in the privacy of the family kitchen. Most female Western visitors to these households come away amazed at the freedom and ease with which Arab-world women enjoy the sexiest of dances with each other at home. There is no shame in this, and their delight is completely infectious. It is perhaps easier because men and women remain more discreetly dressed and so it is possible to be very sensual without giving mistaken impressions that this is an immediate prelude to sexual activity. Indeed, the young children, both girls and boys, are strongly encouraged to join into these times for dancing. And when the men show up for the celebration they may join into the dancing and express the same range of sensual movement.

Westerners who had previously been exposed to mythologies about the "repression of Arab-world women" come away with their jaws dropping. It's a rare grandmother in North America who comes up with moves like these to teach her little five-year-old grand-daughters! When people of all ages are encouraged to open fully to "sacred flirtation" everyone breathes a tremendous sigh of relief. Life feels full and honest once again. Nothing major is being repressed. Dangerous situations develop when strong energies are repressed. They will find a way to suddenly explode outwardly in unpredictable ways.

Once we are exposed to the comfort with which this deep sensuality is expressed in much of the Arab world, we take another look at our own, supposedly liberated culture, and we begin to see the awkwardness which we have inherited. North American or European dancers, many of them now quite excellent, have had to deal with the fact that there was no sexy grandmother in their kitchen and have had to import their moves from somewhere else. They can, of course, look within themselves and find them there. Middle Eastern dance is frequently called the most natural dance in the world. But a few classes with another belly dancer help get people into the flow.

Looking at the ways we habitually express our sensuality in the West we begin to notice that there is frequently a forced kind of over-drive dance of almost athletic sexuality displayed in the movies and in theater which is entertaining but is not for everyone... we notice that there is a coldness in the ways the professional models move... we notice that most Western men are hopelessly out of touch with ways to move to music and express a truly liquid sensuality... we notice that there is a pornographic culture which thrives on perpetrating a very violent attitude toward women...

What happened to a very natural gentle and easy movement in sensuality befitting the energies of an eternal goddess? We look the world over and we find this strongly alive and well in the Arab world!

Of course there are fundamentalist types who disapprove of everything which does not concern itself with the worship of a God perceived to be male. Political and religious leaders, vying for power and control over peoples' lives, immediately adopt a jealous and judgmental stance toward our ancient inalienable rights to enjoy sacred flirtation. We find this in both the East and the West. Fortunately, they generally remain a small minority. But the way some modern Western journalists like to focus on these elements of Islamic society frequently misleads Westerners into thinking that they are the norm.

When I look into the eyes of Arab-world women whom I pass on the street, I feel a strong energy arising from their souls which tells me that they are used to being loved very deeply. And it tells me that they live in a society which is structured in such a way as to make it safe for them to engage in deep "sacred flirtation." Where and when they do this follows a different set of rules from those in the West, but there are obviously places for most of them to be in deep comfort with their extreme femininity.

When we watch Arab-world families and relatives and friends together at a restaurant, we frequently see them enjoying a tremendous delight with each other. They are not as guarded as are Westerners who tend to equate flirtation with aggressive behavior. It is in some ways harder for us to find that safe zone in which our energetic attractions can feel completely natural. But still, every human society must find its own ways for the expression of "Sacred Flirtation." It is as ancient as life itself.

Dina has performed her belly dancing role in Egypt for many years as a "Goddess of Sacred Flirtation."
Men, women and children all feel a deep comfort in her presence.

Musical Enlightenment and Ecstasy

We all must have access to ecstatic vibrations to effectively channel our own creative energies. Musicians and dancers frequently find, during the course of their careers, that they have frequent opportunities to escape the relentless rounds of thought which become so tiresome in our minds.

By entering the trance of "playing" instruments or "becoming" a dance, we have an easy way to allow the verbal components of our beings to fall silent. A musician can sometimes pick up an instrument and within 10 minutes become lost in a spontaneous composition which is made of textures of sound and nothing else. I'm not really talking about playing music by reading it from a piece of paper. But by just picking up an instrument and listening to its sounds as we "make love to it," we can easily take a break from our own word-based mental stream of consciousness and that allows deeper energies to pass through us which have a deep cleansing action. Musicians and dancers and meditators have a similar path toward freedom from endless internal dialogues and, eventually, toward inner silence.

When a pair or group of people allow their dancing bodies to communicate and give form to "sacred flirtation" they can easily enter places where the verbal mental process falls away to be replaced by the sheer delight of initiating symmetrical motion. Some psychologists call this "entrainment" and acknowledge the magic and power of this practice. A spontaneous dance can also interrupt the usual thinking-in-words-only patterns and allow entrance into energetically effortless realms. And once we have entered, we don't go back. The place of peace which exists in all of us but which is beyond our "selves" eternally calls to us to lay down our minds and let the pure light flow through us.

Personal Mental Growth

Stretch, crunch, ouch, pain...
No no no...
I'm sure I already know know know...
so so so...
...so many true and wonderful things...
but...
Why am I still sometimes scared and sometimes angry?
...if I can just get up over this last mountain...
I'll be able to see the whole world...

These Peruvian musicians frequently alternate playing each single note in their songs. This makes it a very tribal activity. You could say that "one person with six arms" is playing the three pan-pipes in this picture. I have seen them dance and play in the same circle for an entire day during local village festivals.

.

Working against Arrogance
sorry, it's not so easy...

After spending 8 years during my twenties traveling back and forth between Colorado and Peru, I found myself strangely uncomfortable with so many things in North America. I had acquired a Spanish-speaking soul and an Inca-speaking soul. After eight years of coming and going from the Andean region, I discovered that no matter which village I passed through in Southern Peru, I ran into Quechua (Inca) Indian people whom I knew from somewhere or another. I had an ongoing social life which involved everything from helping families farm their mountainsides to carrying medicines to remote places to showing up for four-day music and dance parties.

Because I had begun to internalize the rhythms, melodies and lyrics of their village songs, I felt like a part of things when people would sing and dance and play. And when we sat up all night singing the soulful laments about the loneliness of life high in the mountains with sometimes nothing but the sound of one's own flute, I found that I shared this emotional reality with my Inca friends. We would make impromptu speeches to honor our friendship, which had grown out of nowhere, and pledge eternal allegiance to our combined spirits. Sometimes in the afternoons I would hike high above the village in which I was living and meditate in my own special personally chosen magnetic spot facing the mirror-like surface of a distant rock face thousands of feet across the valley.

My Inca friends were living their lives on a day-to-day survival level, planting potatoes and herding sheep as had dozens of generations of their forefathers. Twice I was there when one of the more elderly villagers was found sitting frozen beside the trail. This seemed to be one of the ways their spirits would commonly depart: while resting alone high above a massive Andean valley. I noticed that families would mourn their departed elders, but their comments did not indicate to me that death was a particularly fearful thing for them. It was not that they were any less attached to life or that they enjoyed life any less than we do here in North America... it was more that fear was a luxury they had never been able to afford.

They thought nothing of covering 20 mile distances crossing 16,000 foot passes with 100-pound sacks of potatoes on their backs. I have never been around people anywhere who come close to matching their physical strength. They lived largely outside the monetary economy and conducted the majority of their transactions through trade. The more time I spent in their company, the more I found myself relaxing into a basically human rhythm of life. Upon returning to America and our concerns with insurance policies, motorized toys and leisure-time activities, I felt increasingly like a fish out of water. My home culture appeared to me as being a lot about "having things" and then "being afraid of losing things."

Every time I returned to Peru, I was able to bathe in an ancient civilization which seemed relatively free of fear. That was what I noticed: the time spent worrying in North America could be spent working toward the common good of your family and village in South America.

I realized that I, too, had a personal choice I could make. Would I rather worry or work? Even my Inca friends' six-year-old children were already busy planting, cooking and traveling to accomplish family errands... And they seemed so relaxed and so capable of feeling the basic joys of life: sharing hospitality in their homes and selling oranges from their market kiosks.

Now when I travel in the Arab-speaking world I can't help but notice the directness with which people share their concerns for producing an egalitarian society, which has, in spite of many ups and downs, been a constant Islamic goal. Instant democratic tribunals spring up on street corners to settle disputes; people seem more interested in justice than in labyrinths of lawyer-induced technicalities... How much can we learn from cultures such as these?

Returning from Inca lands to North America I would stare in disbelief at the back cover of Time Magazine: there were the faces of the children who lived in such "poverty" in Third World villages. The photographers, I supposed, had had a hard time finding a child who wasn't grinning ear to ear and having a good time with life. The magazine ads beseeched Americans to send money to funds dedicated to "taking these poor children off the streets..." I had been living with people who were "starving" by North American standards. Yet these "starving" people were energetically thriving. True famine does exist in the world, usually as a result of a kind of warfare wherein one tribe literally works to starve out another. This has been happening in Ethiopia, Rwanda and the Sudan. But this is not what was happening in Peru and Bolivia.

There are many truly humanitarian efforts being made by Christian missionaries in many parts of the globe. And I have met Jesuit Catholics who have developed deep knowledge of indigenous peoples and worked very beautifully in harmony with them. Unfortunately, I have also seen some missionary efforts which did not look so healthy to me. I feel that I should mention these instances in order to encourage others to look twice before they offer support for all so-called philanthropic work.

I once visited and a Christian missionary compound on the shore of Lake Titicaca where priests from Missouri boasted to me about how good it had felt to them to punch Inca Indians in the face to "teach them a lesson." I was horrified to think that huge amounts of dollars were being sent to support "education" of villagers' children by these strangely puritanical North American missionaries. I watched them deliver a midnight mass on Christmas Eve. No longer wearing their Army fatigues, in which they preferred to lounge when not in the pulpit, they stood in golden robes with tall pointed hats in front of an audience of sleepy-looking Indians and chastised them with angry tones for "not knowing what it means to treat each other as brothers." Back in North America I felt virtually alone. No one else in the United States, it seemed, had actually witnessed what some of these missionaries were doing. And no one else, it seemed, had spent years wandering the streets and villages of indigenous peoples in Latin America learning to appreciate how gorgeous, in many ways, their existence is!

North Americans were being programmed to "feel sorry" for all these beautiful Native American children so that our relatively coarse materialistic society could make inroads into their lands and begin raising their children! I had visited another missionary camp in the Amazon basin where pilots descended like gods from the sky in small airplanes, landing on the rivers and enticing the local Native Americans to cut the jungle back to nothing and plant Kentucky bluegrass on the wetlands. The local Indians could be seen working behind the imported lawn-mowers or in the missionaries' kitchens. How unhappy they looked in these roles.

My soul shrank with shame as I realized what my culture was up to. I kept returning to an America filled with well-meaning people who "wanted to help" the poor people on the rest of the planet without realizing that it was our culture which was in desperate need of learning wisdom from them! Americans would open their mouths and their language would speak about the so-called pity felt for other cultures that lived in greater material poverty and what was really going on was that the way was being prepared for another invasion by our fear-driven ways of life! Islamic women have watched over and over again as European, and now American, armies are willing to come and bomb their countries to "liberate" them! Our governments seem to even succeed in convincing our citizens that we are bombing these Muslim countries "for their own good!"

The same American readers who casually glance over endless articles covering the incredible domestic violence which exists inside our own country will turn the page and find an article which helps them grieve about the supposed misery of our distant sisters in the Middle East. It's such a strong pattern that I have come to mistrust expressions of pity or "feeling sorry for" third world people. Is it true compassion or is it another excuse for invasion?

Perhaps I just happen to have bad luck with missionaries. During the early 1990's, working in computer-aided-design fields, I was hired as a contractor by a company in Colorado which outfits helicopters so they can be used in medical emergencies. I was assigned to help outfit two huge jets with hospital and dental equipment for a very well-known Christian evangelist organization. At first we were told that these planes, funded by contributions from America's churches, would be used to help bring medical aid to African villagers. They were to become "flying hospitals." Initially, I felt proud to be working on such a humanitarian project.

My job was to create technology for mobile dental equipment to be held in place during take-offs and landings. Halfway through the project I was told by my bosses that all I really needed to do was design a huge box for everything to be put it in the aircraft's cargo hold *because it would never really be unpacked and used anyway.* Rumors filtered down through the company that the leading evangelist in charge of the organization had been given mineral rights somewhere in Africa and that these planes, while pretending to be flying hospitals, would actually be used to secretly fly diamonds and diamond mining equipment. So I finished the design job and was re-assigned to help figure out how to fit oxygen tanks into helicopters.

I forgot about the whole thing until about ten years later when a small article in a newspaper caught my eye. It was about a pilot who had decided to tell the truth about his job in Africa. He had gone to the press and made a public confession: under the pretense of bringing medical care to remote villagers in Africa, he had for several years flown missions associated with clandestine and illegal mining operations on behalf of this same evangelical organization and had only once delivered a small package of medicines. Just as we had suspected, the "flying hospitals" had been nothing more than a false front! Meanwhile, back in America, well-meaning Christians continued to shell out their donations to support this so-called mission of mercy.

"No, no!" my soul sometimes cries inside. There is so much unconscious arrogance in the common phrases of modern American English! We talk about alleviating poverty out of one side of our mouths and then assume it is right for our banks to charge impossibly high interest rates on loans to people in poverty.

It came as a shock to me to discover that in the Arab Muslim world to this day that charging any interest at all on a loan is still considered to be "usury." Ideally, when Muslims lend money they do so because they believe in the project they are funding and there is no "interest" on the loan. There is an understanding that someone on the receiving end of a loan will, when it becomes possible, make the lender a partner in return for the favor. One of the pillars of Islam is a mandate for alms-giving: giving money directly to the poor. And it appears that most Islamic people actually carry this out. One sees very few homeless people on their streets compared to what we see in many American cities. Here in America, I have come to learn, the wealthy grow fatter off the "interest" charged on money lent. "It takes money to make money," as they say. And we are supposed to feel that Muslims are lucky as Western banking systems continue to gain toeholds in their economies! Indeed today, the true Islamic banks are being outnumbered by the Western banks and customs are changing. More and more Muslim people are also becoming money-lenders.

It's not until you buy your language books and your tickets and go and visit other parts of the world that you can discover, on a level that means something to your very being, on a level that means something in the depths of your soul, that our way of life doesn't look so shiny in any but a material way. We are obsessed with "exporting" the American way when we are desperately in need of "importing" ancient wisdoms from all over the world.

Other peoples and other civilizations have ways of honoring women, "worshipping the feminine," as we call it; ways of raising children so that they are genuinely concerned with justice, and ways of minimizing violence and theft that in many ways work much more elegantly than the equivalents in our society. There are also ways, of course, in which every society on earth does *not* work so elegantly, but it will be by combining our different wisdoms that humankind will eventually have hope for creating a world we are all proud to share!

Warm Spot
They arrive on horseback from the jungle valleys...
They arrive in small boats at the pier...
They arrive in trucks from the distant mountain passes...
It's three o'clock in the morning
A small shack in the marketplace serves hot coffee and bread
Many languages are spoken
We're all glad to be here

(Written at 3:00 a.m. in a giant outdoor food marketplace in Lima, Peru in the summer of 1973)

A family of musicians in Egypt.

'Civilization' – Whose?

'Civilization' may mean more than having access to credit cards and hamburgers. In an atmosphere of greater wisdom, we would draw on lessons learned from and values held by the thousands of civilizations which have graced our planet in the last 20,000 years. Ironically, it is almost always the most barbaric tribe who, in its uneducated ignorance, thinks that it is "leading" the world into a more advanced stage of civilization. The attempts of the gentler, more enlightened tribes, who have accomplished methods of living in peace with each other and who have little need for developing military might, to reason with the more barbaric civilization are always misunderstood.

The more barbaric civilization usually translates everything into a "you are either with us or you are against us" formula and consequently brings the power of its superior military might to subjugate the more enlightened ones. This is apparently what happened when Ghengis Khan "brought civilization" and slaughtered close to one million citizens of Baghdad in the middle of the 13th century. This is also clearly what happened when the Portuguese "brought civilization" and invaded the Indian Ocean and disrupted the ways of the vast Gujarati and Arabic civilization who were peacefully doing business with each other in the 16th century as they had been for hundreds of years. Having traveled recently in the Arab-speaking world and been afforded the opportunity, especially because of the musical connection, to see their ways of egalitarian communication, I am ashamed to say that this pattern is appearing again as the Americans "bring civilization" to the Arab world. Are we, again, revealing ourselves to be the barbarians from the North?

The following excerpts describe the nature of the vast trading empire which extended from the west coast of India to the Arab World in the 12th through the 16th centuries. It appears that a very civilized society existed from the Indian Ocean to Egypt and beyond into the Mediterranean. Again, like the Mongol hordes from the North, the Europeans arrived, also from the North, and disrupted this relatively peaceful world.

Much of the history of the ways people lived in the vast Indian Ocean, Arab and Mediterranean world trading empire is compiled from the study of records kept in a very old synagogue in Cairo which contained records kept by Jewish merchants for the last thousand years.

A bare two years after Vasco da Gama's first voyage to the West Coast of India in 1498, a Portuguese fleet led by Pedro Alvarez Cabral arrived on that same Malabar coast. Cabral delivered a letter from the king of Portugal to the Hindu ruler of the city-state of Calicut, demanding that he expel all Muslims from his kingdom as they were enemies of the 'Holy Faith'. He met with a blank refusal; then, as afterwards, the Hindu ruler steadfastly maintained that Calicut had always been open to everyone who wished to trade there – the Portuguese were welcome to as much pepper as they liked, so long as they bought it at cost price. The Portuguese fleet sailed away, but not before Calicut had been subjected to a two-day bombardment. A year or so later Vasco da Gama returned with another, much more powerful Portuguese fleet and demanded once again that all Muslim traders be expelled from Calicut.

During those early years the peoples who had traditionally participated in the Indian Ocean trade were taken completely by surprise. In all the centuries in which it had flourished and grown, no state or king or ruling power had ever before tried to gain control of the Indian Ocean trade by force of arms. The territorial and dynastic ambitions that were pursued with such determination on land were generally not allowed to spill over into the sea.

Within the Western historiographical record the unarmed character of the Indian Ocean trade is often represented as a lack, or failure, one that invited the intervention of Europe, with its increasing proficiency in war. When a defeat is as complete as was that of the trading cultures of the Indian Ocean, it is hard to allow the vanquished the dignity of nuances of choice and preference. Yet it is worth allowing for the possibility that the peaceful traditions of the oceanic trade may have been, in a quiet and inarticulate way, the product of a rare cultural choice – one that may have owed a great deal to the pacifist customs and beliefs of the Gujarati, Jains and Vanias who played such an important part in it. At the time, at least one European was moved to bewilderment by the unfamiliar mores of the region; a response more honest perhaps than the trust in historical inevitability that has supplanted it since. 'The heathen [of Gujarat]', wrote Tomes Pires, early in the sixteenth century, 'held that they must never kill anyone, nor must they have armed men in their company. If they were captured and [their captors] wanted to kill them all, they did not resist. This is the Gujarat law among the heathen.'

It was because of those singular traditions, perhaps, that the rulers of the Indian Ocean ports were utterly confounded by the demands and actions of the Portuguese. Having long been accustomed to the tradesman's rules of bargaining and compromise, they tried time and time again to reach an understanding with the Europeans – only to discover, as one historian has put it, that the choice was 'between resistance and submission; cooperation was not offered.' Unable to compete in the Indian Ocean trade by purely commercial means, the Europeans were bent on taking control of it by aggression, pure and distilled, by unleashing violence on a scale unprecedented on those shores. As far as the Portuguese were concerned, they had declared a proprietorial right over the Indian Ocean: since none of the peoples who lived around it had thought to claim ownership of it before their arrival, they could not expect the right of free passage in it now.

By the time the trading nations of the Indian Ocean began to realize that their old understandings had been rendered defunct by the Europeans it was already too late. In 1509 AD the fate of that ancient trading culture was sealed in a naval engagement that was sadly, perhaps pathetically, evocative of its ethos: a transcontinental fleet, hastily put together by the Muslim potentate of Gujarat, the Hindu ruler of Calicut, and the Sultan of Egypt was attacked and defeated by a Portuguese force off the shores of Diu, in Gujarat. As always, the determination of a small, united band of soldiers triumphed easily over the rich confusions that accompany a culture of accommodation and compromise.

The battle proved decisive; the Indian and Egyptian ships were put to flight and the Portuguese never again had to face a serious naval challenge in the Indian Ocean until the arrival of the Dutch. Soon, the remains of the Indian Ocean Trading civilization were devoured by that unquenchable, demonic thirst that has raged ever since, for almost five hundred years, over the Indian Ocean, the Arabian Sea and the Persian Gulf.[5]

Similarly, we must note, it wasn't until the arrival of the British and the French in the 1920's, that "ownership" was claimed in the Middle East and geographical boundaries were drawn on the earth and Saudi Arabia, Jordan, Syria, Iraq and, later, Israel, were created. And, as we have seen, another delicate balance was hopelessly upset. And again we must ask ourselves who are the real barbarians?

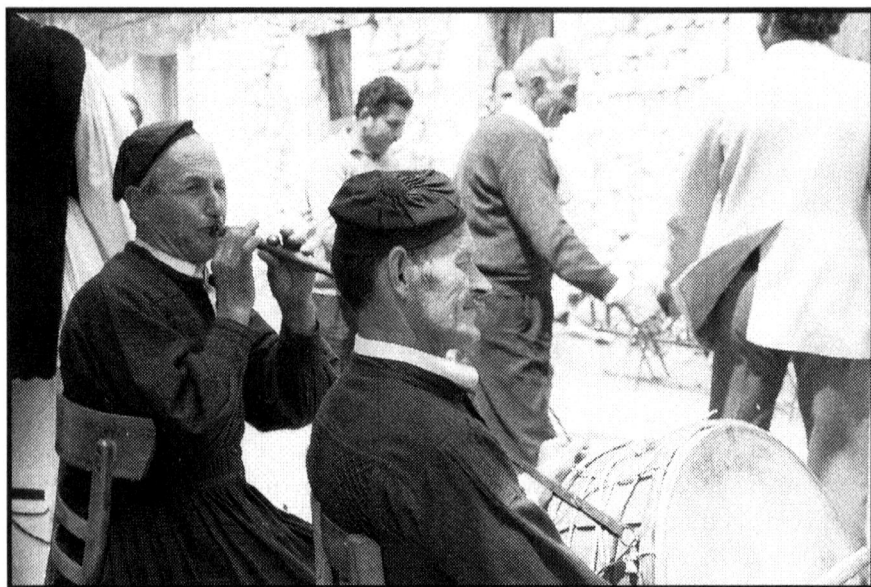

Greek villagers celibrate a moment of freedom with a dance.

Photo by Yvonne Derrer

Why Working for Peace is not Enough

Whose Peace is it anyway?

The invaders?

The invaded?

The neighbors who have to keep helping the invaders and the invaded?

The neighbors who are tired of having the fighting in their back yard?

The yogi in his cave?

The American thousands of miles away from conflicts in his living room or church or meditation hall?

Each one of these takes for granted that their idea of peace is a complete solution.

As a musician who works for peace, I receive numerous suggestions about what songs I should sing. I realized many years ago that different languages espouse different ideas of "peace."

A culture which just invaded an indigenous land may sing endlessly about their idea of "peace," which may simply be that they wish that the native people whom they have just displaced would end their resistance and quietly accept subjugation.

The invaded people, however, will be singing an antithetical type of "peace" song. Their concept of peace, obviously, will be that the invaders will pack up their bags and go back to wherever they came from.

Meanwhile, the culture next door, who is accommodating whole generations of refugees displaced by the neighboring invasion, will sing a song of "peace" in which they can be left alone to return to their original tribal business.

If I were to accept singing a "peace" song from any of these cultures, I would, in effect, simply be choosing sides in a conflict. That's not my own personal idea of peace.

About thirty years ago I had stationery printed with the names of every "country" in the world printed faintly in the background. Then I typed requests to forty or so "ministries of culture" for whom I could find addresses in a multitude of countries around the world for tapes of their popular folk music. I explained that I had a band which was devoted to playing popular music from all around the world. I received replies and tapes from about ten of these different countries. I listened to them all and I eventually learned to sing some of these tunes. One of them immediately stuck out: it was a so-called "peace" song. It was built on the rhythm of a military march! I immediately realized that this was one "peace" song which I would not be learning. "Marching toward peace" is something we can do when we want to combat prejudiced legal systems or unjust governments. Motivated by anger, we can, and must, at times do this.

But there is another peace which we must not forget to cultivate: the one referred to in the world's great love songs. I discovered long ago that I cannot sing beautiful love songs if my dominant internal emotion is anger! Many of the world's so-called "peace" songs carry undercurrents of anger. These are perhaps better labeled "revolutionary" songs. It is fine to sing revolutionary songs when one is part of a revolution, but we should not think that we are singing peace songs. The great artists and lovers are pointing in another direction with their music and art: towards a path of surrender to the beloved. It is in the flavors of this music and art that we find genuine moods of peace.

Personal Soul Growth: Becoming a World Citizen

Something in me is breathing at last!
I feel like I am finally home!

*Yannis, who lives on the southern shore of the island of Crete,
is one of those who took the time and trouble to help
stretch my soul early in life.*

Photo by Yvonne Derrer

Gain a New Soul by Entering a New Culture

As you learn a new language you gain a new soul.

As we begin to understand the incredible vehicle for personal spiritual growth which is offered by this path of traveling as "reverse missionaries" wherein our goal is to learn from the beautiful ancient civilizations on this planet and offer nothing more nor less than our hearts, and we begin to be able to carry on rudimentary conversations in another language, we will at some point realize that we have acquired a new little baby soul which speaks that language!

I will never forget standing on an Andean hillside above a Peruvian village several hours into the evening's musical festival, opening my mouth and listening to myself exclaim: "Que bonita la luna esta brillando en el cielo!" (See how beautiful is the moon on this night!) ...in Spanish! It was the first time I heard myself spontaneously speak in a language other than English without having to go through the mental translation process. A little baby three-year-old Spanish-speaking soul was born inside me in that moment and for the rest of my life it has craved interaction and growth in Spanish! As that soul slowly matures it gains wisdom, not in English terms, but in its own language! And as I learned to sing in other languages, those other new souls sprout blossoms, bear fruit and begin to sway in the warm breezes of those new climates! There is actually hope for becoming an embodiment of accumulated wisdom from multiple civilizations and for feeling yourself dancing in the wind currents of all those peoples and places!

But this kind of soul acquisition can have some very painful expansion periods. We feel ourselves being stretched. We have to gradually surrender our national identity and let go of many ways of doing things which we took for granted as we passed through childhood in our home countries.

In order for me to begin to feel at home in Greece where many things "American" were seen as naive, I had to go through painful changes. I wasn't convinced that Greeks had all the correct answers, but I had to learn that my own impulsive defenses of "things American" were equally untrustworthy. It took years to let go of enough of my own structure to become a more flexible being capable of knowing "that we are all right from our own points of view." Then I could succumb to the ultimately humorous reality of that truth.

And, of course, the stretching has only just begun!

Fellow performers at a peace concert in Omaha, Nebraska.

Enlightenment and Inner Peace
...in these times?
...with all this noise?

My Egyptian friend Nasser, who owns a music shop in central Cairo, always greets me with an hour of tea-drinking and gentle music which he plays softly on one of his ouds. He maintains a personal demeanor of deep peace while hundreds of horns honk outside his store and he simultaneously handles dozens of complex phone calls and business transactions. Nasser seems to maintain an inner peace.

All across America we have been met by warm people who have taken the time to invite us to come and give one of our presentations. We have been hosted by hundreds of wonderful folks who have offered their unlocked homes and their unlocked hearts one after another as we travel. They make these offerings out of a quiet unspoken trust and take the time to create personal welcome mats woven from the rich fabrics of their lives and the peaches in their kitchens and offer them to us. These offerings are extended by individuals who have found some enlightenment and inner peace in these times.

*Sisters and cousins in Syria have invited us for a meal
and an evening of singing.
Ancient family values and elegant interactions between family members
of all ages bring to life their reputation for hospitality.*

No Humor at the Expense of Others

When my kids were little I was building houses. My friends were other carpenters, and we excelled in the art of insulting each other.

As you watch your partner struggle to pour another 94-pound sack of concrete into the mixer toward the end of the day you laugh at his exhaustion and exclaim loudly to another carpenter: "%$#@ing child labor! That's all you can find around here anymore!"

"I'm going to pour the next bag down your throat!" retorts your partner. We all laughed together because we were all in the same bubble of work-induced camaraderie.

I thought this humor was grand and soon my own children were trying to learn to find it funny to make such overstated fun of others, who supposedly always knew that it was 'just a joke'. I watched my children struggle with mastering this art at school. It's not entirely easy and it's possible to accidentally hurt people's feelings when they don't know that you are trying to include them in the same "bubble of camaraderie."

After a few years I had an opportunity to sell one of the construction companies and go into children's television. We actually won a regional 'Emmy Award' for a program called "The Bug Hollow Show."

We used puppets and we wrote scripts for small children wherein humor at the expense of others was carefully avoided. We thought young children were being exposed to too much violence even in cartoons displayed on television. Our characters laughed when something *good* happened and the only obstacles they faced were the results of confusion brought about by the well-intended but frequently naive actions of certain goofy characters.

We had developed our scripts by performing hundreds of puppet shows for local children's birthday parties and for kindergarten and pre-school classes. We witnessed the small children melt into our shows and our characters because there was nothing threatening there. It was an uplifting experience for them and for their parents. But after all was said and done, we had to admit that our live performances had actually been much better than the staged ones captured by the $100,000 worth of professional video crews donated by the local center for performing arts.

Why was this? It was largely because every day we faced an uphill battle with the cameramen who filmed our puppets who continually assumed that humor primarily arose when pain was experienced by one of the characters. They were trying to include our puppets in their jovial "bubble of camaraderie." When a puppet falls on its face you are supposed to laugh! That is the nature of the cartoons we have been raised on. We have learned to think making fun of other people and other cultures is a key ingredient for humor! This comes complete with lots of human imitations of airplane and machine-gun sounds! But this "bubble of camaraderie" was not going to really include the audience of TV-watching 3-year-olds for whom our show was intended. Their natural tendency, with a few exceptions, is to cringe when they see this violent kind of humor.

So every day we were saying to the cameramen: "Ok guys, now let's try and get back to what this scene is really about!"

In the Peruvian Inca world and in the Arab World, do our American cartoon jokes arouse laughter? They don't always seem to. Sometimes they arouse blank stares. I once talked a village Peruvian into coming to see a movie with me while we were in a large town. He brought his older children with him, but I soon noticed him covering their eyes with his hands every time a supposedly "funny" event happened! He wouldn't have understood what's so funny about a puppet falling on its face. Arab comedy shows tend to feature loud-mouthed "fools" who, impervious to how ridiculous they appear, in the end are proven to have had an idiotic "wisdom" which makes the audience think twice. Nasrudin, the famous Sufi "village idiot" plays out this role in the Islamic world. People laugh, but something of value about human morality is simultaneously learned. An elderly American man recently commented to me that he didn't think it was until after WWII that "humor at the expense of others" arose to become so popular in our culture.

It took me a few years, after our experience with filming the children's videos, to unlearn my own habits of relying on humor at the expense of others. It was tough to break it, but I eventually succeeded in freeing myself of this strange habit. The reward is that verbal space became freed up in my mind to allow myself to ponder more interesting paths of thought! Now I seldom risk accidentally offending others and can move more widely through different segments of society. And hopefully my children have been able to witness their own father's evolution into a place beyond "humor at the expense of others."

Also, clearly, we should not create or play violent video or war games, nor watch violent "entertainment." To watch or play them contributes toward making this violence seem acceptable.

Our personal soul growth can happen more easily if we gradually wean ourselves of many violent forms of entertainment which our culture deems perfectly acceptable.

The dualistic "us vs. them" reality to which we become habituated when we learn humor at the expense of others evolves into the equally fallacious and dualistic dogmas related to seeing human beings as "good vs. evil."

There is a greater viewpoint which we can experience when we become truly free spirits. This viewpoint is beyond "good and evil" and from there we see all beings with compassion. Tragically, although the prophets and sages point us in this direction, the religious institutions created by their followers in their names acquire heavy weights which pull their followers back into the delusional worlds of "good vs. evil."

This makes spiritual progress doubly difficult. First, it requires work to gain the compassion required to imagine ourselves wearing every possible pair of shoes or moccasins. Secondly, we have to learn to ignore the "advice" given by supposedly "wise elders" who would have us divide humanity into "us and them" or "the followers of good" vs. "the followers of evil."

Young Muslim Women in Cairo, Egypt.

Becoming the Prayer
No Fear

Be the change you want to see. Walk the pathways beyond the verbal which keep you in constant contact with creative life forces.

Learn to move through your own fears. Prayer is the natural state of compassion which exists between all human beings in the absence of fear.

Greek singers and Iraqi mystics were the ones who first taught me the incredibly sweet arts of singing and dancing in timeless space. When Greeks sing certain songs together, there is absolutely no hurry. An opportunity for complete surrender opens and we take it! When an Iraqi Sufi master moves his body in dance, the movements can be so slow that they could take forever. Another opportunity for complete surrender opens and we take it!

Dissolving into a timeless space of singing or dancing allows the natural state of compassion to arise spontaneously in our beings.

We learn by experience that fear is always an obstacle and gradually we discover that it is nothing more than a "luxury" only affordable by citizens of "first world countries." We become more eager to reclaim our ancient indigenous roots and escape this "luxury."

The richest man is he who needs the least!

The freest man is he who fears the least!

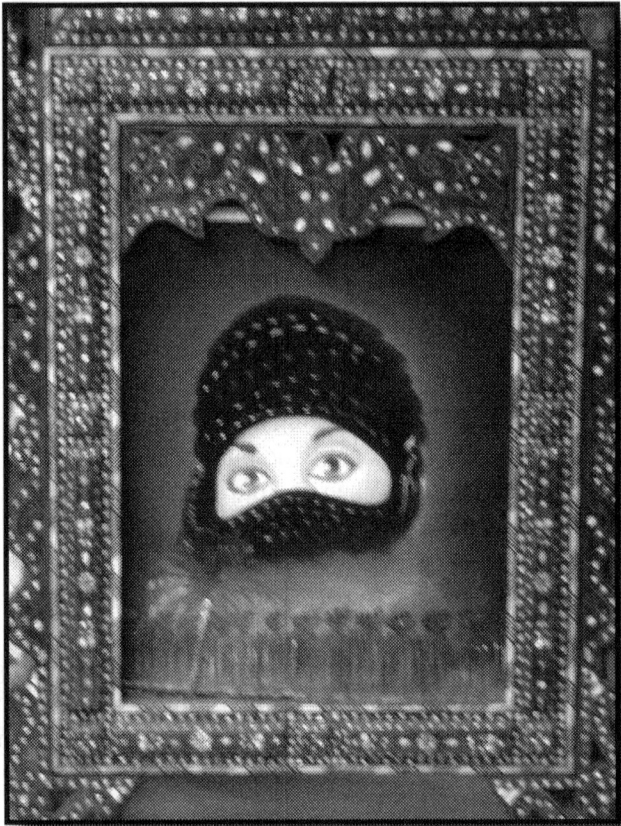

It's not possible to find too fancy a frame for this young Syrian artist's fanciful rendition of "the Goddess."

Worshipping the Feminine in the Middle East and Elsewhere; How does it work?

Being able to see the Garden when you are in it.

Kristina and I were both reading different articles about Islamic women the other evening. While I was reading one which made the claim that women took a large fall in value with the advent of Islam, Kristina was reading another article making the opposite claim: that Islam was responsible for a huge expansion of women's rights in the seventh century.

But who are Muslim women really? We know that, like women the world over, they are emitting a sacred perfume. Men are being attracted by and welcomed into this perfume in the Muslim world just as they are in every other part of the world. "Sacred flirtation" is always in the subtle smoke of male-female human relations.

Who are these Muslim women really? And who are the Muslim men who become their husbands? Why is the music and dance from the Arab world so sensual? Why have Europeans been endlessly fascinated by this "Oriental" magnetism?

It is a mistake to look into Islam to explain everything. Long before the arrival of Islam, the people from the Nile valley had a special flavor. The people from the Tigris and Euphrates river valleys had a special flavor. The people from the eastern Mediterranean shore had a special flavor. They were not all called Egyptians and they were not all called Iraqis and they were not all called Lebanese or Palestinians or Syrians. Those countries, as we have seen, were created by modern European map-makers.

If we want to know who "Islamic" women really are and want to know how the subtle and mysterious sources of their various "psychic perfumes," we will want to be close up to them so that we can absorb the essences of truly ancient forms of femininity.

Records of ancient "Musical Missionaries" are fascinating to read.

Sometimes they reveal attitudes toward women. Fatema Mernissi quotes Ibn 'Arabi, born in Murcia (Spain) in 560 of the Hijra (1165 of the Christian calendar) and makes further comments of her own:

As for the Sufis and women, it is no wonder that male Sufis celebrate femininity as energy, an opportunity for men to blossom and thrive. For Ibn 'Arabi, the female lover is "tayyar" or, literally, endowed with wings, an idea that the Muslim miniature painters often tried to capture. Sufi men seem to explore the subconscious of the Muslim psyche where myths and legends, sacred and profane, endow women with extraordinary powers. From the dazzling Queen of Sheba to the irresistible Zuleikha in the sacred Koran, to horse-riding Shirin in the Persian legends and the subversive Scheherazade in Arabic tales, to modern women artists today, the feminine stands as a challenge in Islamic art. This brings us to understand better why intellectually dazzling female Al-Jazeera television hosts enchant male viewers.

We can read modern comments: Fahmy Huweidi, who is a widely read and highly respected moderate Egyptian Muslim writer and scholar, and a man, comments:

I do not think that the Arab woman is better off, but, I believe that the European woman is even more miserable and wretched. Comparative statistics on the rates of suicide, the numbers of destroyed families, injuries at the hands of fugitives, criminals, and drug addicts all clearly indicate that Arab women have a higher percentage of stability and higher level of personal safety than their counterparts from the West. Of all the errors committed by many Westerners, and some Muslims, too, the worst by far has been to hold up the model of the Western woman as better and more advanced.

Reading this, what have we learned? Nothing, really, other than that we need to go and see for ourselves!

It is impossible to objectively say whether Western women are better off than Islamic women. It depends on your sets of values. People in the West think Western women are better off. People in the East think Eastern women are better off.

To make the subject more confusing, there are some fraudulent writings circulating in America right now on the subject. The three books which claim to be written by a "Saudi Princess" which purport to describe the misery of life for females in Saudi Arabia were actually written, it turns out, by an Austrian women who worked twenty years ago in a compound for Western workers in

Saudi Arabia. Women in Saudi Arabia are buying these books to laugh at all the mistaken information. For details on this see the article by K. J. Mushung Published in May/June, 2004 issue of Zaghareet Magazine: "Anti-Muslim Sentiment Masquerades As Concern for Women in 'Princess' Trilogy."

What we *can* do to really get to know who Arab-world women are, is to befriend some of them and ask their opinions! This can be done either here in America or in the Arab World. Becoming a Musical Missionary makes it possible to also sing with them!

During our recent travels in the Arab world I did meet one Syrian woman who expressed a desire to immigrate to America so that she could "pursue the American dream." But she was the only one I met who expressed anything other than a deep pride in being part of current Islamic culture.

As I said before, when I walk down the streets of Arab-world countries and I look into the eyes of passing women, I see many very open people who are very willing to be part of the universal "sacred flirtation." Even the women I pass who are wearing a veil covering the lower half of their face usually make a warm and welcoming greeting to me with their eyes. They come from a culture where women are very protected, which can be a two-edged sword, as we know. But, if Fahmy Huweidi is correct, women in the Arab world don't have to deal with near the levels of domestic violence, rape and other aggressive behavior so common in America and in Europe and in Israel. And so they are more open to "sacred flirtation."

I asked an American man whom I recently met who had worked in Kuwait if he had noticed this about the women. "No," he replied. "We were instructed by our American bosses to never look into the eyes of the local women." So he missed the whole thing! A tragedy!

Who are the Islamic women? Personally, I have not yet walked the streets of Indonesia, Pakistan, Afghanistan, Iran, Uzbekistan, Dagestan, Chechnya or many other of the dozens of non-Arabic Islamic countries. The women in those places, I'm sure, have their own special fragrances also. But I have walked the streets and visited many households in the Arab World.

Is "worshipping the feminine" a hot topic in bookstores in Cairo? I don't think so. "Reclaiming the energies of the Goddess" is a hot topic here in America. It could be that in the Arab World "worshipping the feminine" has been, while life is not perfect for either women or men, something which has never been lost. Whether Islam is good for women or not can be endlessly debated. But it could well be that the "goddess worship" still powerfully alive in Arabic culture has been there continuously for thousands of years. The civilizations of the fertile crescent and the Nile river delta have roots in the dawn of history when, it is popularly thought, the "balance of power" between men and women was healthier than it became with the advent of Abraham and the "patriarchal religions," Judaism, Christianity and Islam.

The ancient Egyptian pantheon included both a male and a female sky god and both a male and a female earth god. With the advent of the ancient Greek pantheon we notice the deaths of the female sky god and the male earth god. Perhaps they are both still alive and well in the modern Egyptian psyche but Westerners are generally blind to it. The women I see in Syria and Egypt look to me like they feel like they're walking in a beautiful garden. Why is it that we Westerners cannot see the garden? We can, if we're lucky, smell it from a distance. Could it be that we have lost the primordial receptors for seeing the female sky-Goddess and the male earth-God? Could it be that we have lost the ability to see certain gardens even as we wander through them?

I have an Iraqi friend who tells me that every village in Iraq is a different ancient civilization. "Some are still matriarchal; some have always allowed same-sex marriage for both sexes..." he has told me. "Unimaginably diverse lifestyles and ways for men and women to relate are all contained right here in Iraq!"

I have experienced some of this confusing diversity. Generally when I am invited into Islamic, Arab-speaking households, it is expected that I not actually shake hands with the women. To physically touch a woman who is not your wife is not the custom.

But I have also been invited into a household in Egypt where my host's wife and female sisters and cousins snuggled close all around me as we sang popular songs. I mean really, really close. We sat in a big pile on a bed with our bodies intertwined as we sang! This was not a rich man's household and the women seemed constantly to seek smiles and comfortable physical touch. These were not prostitutes. They were wives, cousins, daughters of the family and they had decided, because I could sing with them and because I was alone with them, to be themselves.

I have sometimes heard that Arab-world men must be vigilant about preserving their female family members' chastity because women are such sensual creatures that they can easily lose control if they find themselves alone with a man. I have two young Syrian friends who decided to quit being seen together in public. One is a young man and the other a young woman. They had been enjoying their friendship a lot, going many places together. But they became worried that people would conclude that they were lovers and that this would be a stain on the young woman's reputation.

So I asked a taxi driver friend one night in Jordan whether people would assume that it was the young man or the young woman who might "lose control" and have irresistible romantic urges.

"It is more likely to be the young woman who would lose control and follow the sexual attraction," he said.

Two other men who came from more wealthy classes in Jordan than my Bedouin taxi driver friend joined the conversation and said they felt the opposite:

that it would be more likely for the young man to be the one to lose control and make advances on the female. After an hour of discussion of this complex subject we rose to leave. My taxi driver friend made the last comment: "There is an easy way for all of this to be solved: anal sex..."

People are basically the same the world over: somewhat unpredictable. But if the upper class man is more likely than the upper class woman to lose control and the lower class woman is more likely than the lower class man to lose control, a certain pattern emerges. It is more likely for an upper class man to have a love affair with a lower class woman than for an upper class woman to have an affair with a lower class man. But this would be true for socio-economic reasons as well. I'm sure I will continue to get different answers to the same question from people of different social classes.

Those of us who are Musical Missionaries and who have been attracted to learning Arabic music have a window into the world of romance as it exists between men and women in these parts of the world. When I lived in Greece and learned Greek music I caught strong flavors of Arabic music. It had come to Greece from Anatolia either directly from the Arabic music popular there or through Turkish music which had evolved in tandem with Arabic music during the Ottoman period.

The Greeks called a certain style of this music "tsiftiteli" and were at the same time embarrassed and delighted to dance to it. It was the equivalent of "belly dance" and Greek men would dance "tsiftiteli" with Greek women on the dance floors of the tavernas when the band performed this style. It was not a line dance, but a sexy couple's dance. But it was regarded as foreign: Turkish or Arabic. Greeks loved to give themselves license to do this dance but they always felt obliged to make disparaging comments about it and disclaim it by labeling it "foreign." What a strange schizophrenia! While doing the dance their bodies became ecstatic and their faces radiated magical smiles, but as soon as it was over they predictably felt a necessity to say something negative. "We don't really like to do that dance," they would lie out of the corners of their mouths. "It's a 'Turkish' dance."

Now when I am with Arab-world people I see a love-hate relationship with sexuality too, but the hate part is more superficial and easily ignored. The underlying love of sexuality and sensuality is closer to the surface than it is with people of northern European descent. It doesn't take much to entice Arab-world men and women to dance, especially in Egypt. In public it is considered too "hot" for men and women to dance together. So the men will dance with the men and the women either alone or with other women. But they feel free to channel the natural energy of attraction through members of the same sex. To do this does not imply that they are "homosexual," as it might in the Western World. For Europeans and Americans to enter this requires taking a leap. The atmosphere is thick with "sacred flirtation" and this is what has always drawn Europeans to the Arab World. This is the sensuality which inspired sensual harem fantasy paintings to come out of France in the eighteenth century, although they were more familiar with the Turkish styles than the Arabic ones. Much, of course, of the Anatolian Turkish lifestyle contained essences of the ways of life of the preceding governing Arab Caliphates. To try and separate the "Turkish" from the "Arabic" during the Ottoman period would be a whole other endeavor. But the tradition of investing female dancers with the power to manifest the "sacred flirtations" that are so powerfully in the air spread, possibly from Egypt, through the Arabic, Turkish and, to some extent, the Greek worlds.

Is it true that Catholics in America have more of a reputation for promiscuity than their more puritanical protestant counterparts? What people say is frequently the opposite of what they do. Forbidden fruits grow especially sweet. Fundamentalist Islamic cultures hold beliefs that the attractions between men and women are the stuff of the devil. But that energy is eagerly released once superficial lip service is given to "fearing the devil." It's like fasting by day and then feasting by night, as people do during the Muslim holy month of Ramadan. Only a tiny percentage of truly orthodox believers actually minimize the feast when its time comes. Most thoroughly enjoy the feasting frenzy. Sales of food, especially sweets, actually increase in the Arab World during Ramadan, the "month of fasting."

I have a female friend here in America who defines herself as Saudi Arabian although she grew up in both Saudi Arabia and Pakistan. She moved to America more than twenty years ago enamored by Western ways. She wore the mini-skirts and went to baseball games. She married an American man and eventually, with her small son, became another American statistic: half of us who marry get divorced and she got divorced. She is now re-married to a Tunisian man and she says, "It is such a relief to be back with a man who knows how to love women!" I am not surprised by her comment. But many Americans would be. I am very happy for her and hope that this will remain a good marriage for her.

My experience with "family values" in the Arab-speaking world inclines me to believe that enduring bonds between husbands and wives are more easily maintained there than in America. For all our talk about "family values," I tend to see more open expression of love between parents and their children over there than I see here at home. There is no shame in those cultures around loving your mother and your father, no matter what a child's age. The whole process which American children go through of "rebelling" seems strangely absent from Arab-world families. Young boys and girls alike hug and kiss their mothers and climb all over their fathers. And the pride and love I have seen between many Arab-world married couples has been deeply uplifting.

So what is our Western obsession with thinking that "Islamic" women are so mistreated?

Certainly there are times and places where women, and men also, are abused by controlling religious fundamentalists. Saudi Arabia, Afghanistan and Iran have recently endured oppressive orthodox ruling minorities. We have pockets, such a the Mormon polygamous town in Arizona called Colorado City, of fundamentalism in the West also in which religion is used as an excuse to abuse and control others. I suppose that when people in power find it necessary to abuse those beneath them in order to maintain their positions, they find that it weighs less on their conscience if they can do it 'in the name of God.' For details on Mormon communities living outside the US law, read "Under the Banner of Heaven," by Jon Krakauer. (Doubleday 2003).

There seems to be a trend in the Muslim world however. People there are beginning to make clearer statements about their preference for even a fundamentalist Islamic government over puppet "democratic" regimes installed by the West. The potential for random violence and confusion is turning out to be so much greater under the Western-installed regimes that they are losing local support more rapidly. The American press doesn't give equal voice to these opinions, but a little digging on the internet through international news sources reveals this pattern.

But many Westerners remain convinced that part of our ancient crusade to bring Christendom and "democracy" to the Arab World is to "liberate" the women. Islamic women remember all too well how the British and French acquired a century-long grip on their lands while fueling their invasions with endless talk back home in London and Paris about "liberating Islamic women." This massive delusion in the West that Islamic women are all abused and need "liberating" is now similarly dominant in American thinking. So we must buy our tickets and travel to the Arab World and ask the women what they think about this before we use the pretext of "liberating Islamic women" again as a pretext for bombing more Islamic people.

MEN, WOMEN, MARRIAGE

Frequently we notice the inequality in Islam between women and men regarding marriage. Men may have up to four wives and women are only allowed one husband at a time. The historical roots for this custom are subjects for various theories. The patriarchal attitude is clear: it has to do with maintaining a clear patrilineal passage of inherited wealth along the paternal bloodlines.

It seems that we inherited this way of doing things from the nuclear family farm era which evolved as a way of life in the temperate zones of the northern hemisphere. It wasn't until a man could build a fence around a woman on a nuclear-family farm miles away from other men that he could pass ownership of land patrilinealy. Before that fence was built he had no real way of knowing who the real father of his children was. Before those nuclear-family farms evolved about 7,000 years ago, ownership was a matrilineal affair. And the world was not densely populated enough to create much importance around "ownership" anyway. For more on this read "The Anatomy of Love," by an anthropologist named Helen Fisher. She has studied 800 tribes, numerous other species and marriage statistics collected by the United Nations all over the world since the 1940's and she attempts to answer the questions about what natural human mating patterns *actually have been* and what they *actually are now* as opposed to propagating more assertions about what they *"should be."*

Humans are like all other animal species: lots of things happen somewhere out there in the bushes. Recent scientific research has finally debunked most of the fairy tales about "birds mating for life." They may form "marriages" in the sense that a mated pair will faithfully raise baby birds together year after year, but when scientists finally got around to doing blood tests on the baby birds, they discovered that mama bird, like mamas of all other species we now know, has a habit of mating with varieties of males out there somewhere in the bushes. It turns out that humans, like all other animals, are much more inclined to "serial monogamy" than life-long monogamy. Helen Fisher's conclusions are absolutely fascinating and this book is a must-read for anyone interested in who we *really are*.

Given that men and women do best if not saddled with guilt patterns based on a morality which arose during "patriarchal times" of nuclear family farming, we might regret that any influence whatsoever from the three patriarchal religions, Judaism, Christianity and Islam, still remains in this era wherein women are regaining their ancient economic independence and freedom. But since, we have to admit, there still are strong legacies in huge segments of humanity from these patriarchal religions, we might as well take a look and see some of what they offer to women.

Judaism preserves inheritance, not of material property, but of "Jewishness" itself, along matrilineal lines. In other words, if your mother is Jewish, you are Jewish, even if your father is not.

Christianity evolved more in the Indo-European world than the Semitic world. By the third century AD it became the official religion of Rome. The morality of Christianity evolved hand in hand with European development.

Islam remained at heart a Semitic religion, although it was later adopted, as we have seen, by others. Christians express disapproval at the provision in the Koran which allows men to have four wives. Now I guess at the time, Mohammed meant that men should be allowed to have "only four wives." We have to remember the context. Most contemporary Arab-world citizens believe that having more than one wife is impossible except for the very wealthy, anyway. After all, who could afford to have more than one wife? Other contemporary Muslim thinkers maintain that, even though the Koran specifies that if a man takes more than one wife he must be certain to love and support them equally, this is really an impossibility: a man will always inadvertently favor the newest wife over the previous one, at least for a time, and so the custom should be discontinued in favor of more egalitarian interests.

Others point out that the real cruelty lies in the Western, Christian custom which virtually requires a husband and wife who are no longer feeling well-matched to become enemies and demonize each other and soon it's "divorce time." This results in societies filled with struggling women, many of whom don't have marketplace skills, suddenly finding themselves on the streets, perhaps even while still trying to rear the younger children! Such a hapless woman is now faced with having to find a job and make do with faltering child-support payments, the complete disdain of her former husband and the new wife, and the task, whether she really wants to or not, of landing another man in order to regain her lost affluence.

In Islam, an older wife is basically guaranteed a more honored role in the family. In other words, there are more options in that system for women. The married couple can choose between divorce or, if the wife would prefer, the acceptance of another wife into the picture without the requirement of divorce. An older wife may say to the younger one: "Go ahead! You take him! I've had enough of intimacy with him for one lifetime!" Separate dwellings may be maintained. But if it just so happens that the first wife, who by this time may not be in love with her husband anyway, would just as soon not have to begin life all over again, she can maintain her honored status as wife and mother and not find herself demonized and cast out of the household by a divorce. If she would prefer to divorce and leave, that option is usually a choice which she can make. Now maybe I'm missing something, but it seems to me that, given the sometimes wayward nature of males, Islamic culture is offering women more options than does Western culture. Of course this doesn't help a woman who is still in love with her husband and who has no wish to see her primary relationship disrupted. Nor does it help in a situation where a man acquires a second wife in a distant town, never even telling his first wife, and thereby plays outside the rules. And of course there still exists a basic inequality: if Islamic men can legitimately marry up to four women, when will Islamic women be able to legitimately marry up to four men?

More deeply unhealthy aspects of all three Abrahamic patriarchal religions lie in their common reliance on requiring their adherents to "fear God." If God is love, then why would he or she be frightening? Human beings have their own capacity to evolve into compassionate beings. "Great world religions" which rely on coercion and threats of "damnation" to induce proper behavior on the parts of their adherents have lost something of their greatness. People required to sit outside of themselves and constantly try and measure their own "sins" are hardly able to enjoy their own bodies as individual temples. Humanity will someday evolve into a consciousness that we are challenged by and deserve more than that. Each human lifetime has the potential, given enough true freedom, to become a personal journey to the divine. And no matter how sternly the fundamentalist lawmakers try and rule, the natural course of human events gives birth to many "Sufis," such as Rabia al-Adawiyya, of Basra, Iraq, who advocated "the Way of Love, worshiping God in friendship rather than fear." [6]

We tend to have our minds made up about which systems we prefer. And it has been said that trying to change a belief is as hard as kicking any other entrenched addiction. But as we grope toward the future it would be smart of us to learn from as many ancient traditions as possible and assemble new social realities which benefit from the experiences of all. And we must listen to the women to hear many of these ancient voices. Deep sensitivity and compassion and nurturing come very naturally to women.

MUSICIANS AND DANCERS

As a musician playing Arabic music, I frequently find the greatest joy in the interaction with a dancer. I don't know of another music and dance tradition wherein the tradition of a musician and a dancer becoming one integrated spiritual energy is so deeply revered. This is the attraction of especially the Egyptian styles of music and dance. As I traveled up the Nile a few years ago with a dancer friend of mine, we arrived at a village where she is a frequently honored guest. Musical events tend to spring up when she arrives and this time the party lasted for nine hours.

The musicians were four mizmar players and one drummer. Mizmars are the ancient ancestor of the oboe and the mesmerizing sound they make is the stuff of snake charmers. I was able to take a photograph of the lead mizmar player politely holding a stick against my friend's moving body while she danced so that he would conduct the vibrations of her dance into his music. She in turn became the visual manifestation of his music. In our culture we do the same thing in larger groups: the crowd will dance to the live energy of a band and the energy of the band will increase as the energy of the dancers rises. It is a group phenomenon. We all know and love this celebration of ecstatic energies.

But in Egypt it is traditional to allow attention to focus on one musician and one dancer at a time so that they have an opportunity to create their own unique artistic moment of expression. This is, from my point of view as a musician, a very special time. The most obvious thing is the substance this form can politely give to "sacred flirtation." The natural attractions which are so strong between men and women can be easily and safely expressed. The ways men worship women in the Arab world become very obvious and very accessible. I don't think anyone who has been there to observe the way this manifests at village festivals could escape discovering the depths to which women are worshipped in these cultures. Control-oriented patriarchal and puritanical energies can make it difficult for people of all social classes to directly participate, but everyone feels the magnetism and is drawn on some level to these musical manifestations of female-worshipping energy. In fact, one of the first things we notice in the Arab World is that men and women both dance out their sensuality in ways that frequently appear identical. The fear a Western man would have of appearing "effeminate" does not exist in the same way.

Sometimes free expression of "sacred flirtation" in dance and music goes somewhat underground when fundamentalist controlling energies take governmental command. It took the 1960's here in America to finally throw off some of the armor we had been wearing. And it is ironic that Englishmen from the Victorian age were "ruling" the Arab World during the first half of the 20th century. The distance between what they felt comfortable with expressing and what Egyptian villagers feel comfortable with expressing is huge. Men like Lawrence of Arabia and Sir Richard Burton dared to explore these expressions. The penalties they paid were that the more they absorbed from the Arab World, the more imprisoned they experienced themselves to be in their own cultures.

But as Musical Missionaries we have given ourselves the tools to explore the underground passages from whence the world's love songs are born! Don't hesitate any longer! Follow our Urgent Travel Advisory: Buy a Ticket to the Arab World or some other exotic part of the globe! Especially at this time in history we cannot let fear be our driving motivation!

There is so much love out there!
As Musical Missionaries we learn to bathe in this
and celebrate the attractions which naturally arise
between all men and all women
and between all women and all women
and between all men and all men!
We are drawn like moths to the flames of love and friendship!
But we are fire moths and we cannot be burned!

Egyptian Whirling Dervish

Study of Exotic Music:
Middle Eastern Music as an Example

Now let's assume that you are a musician or that you have decided to become one. Your opportunities as a Musical Missionary have just multiplied. When you walk into a music store you can pick up an instrument and play it a little bit. Perhaps someone who works in the store will play with you or give you a little lesson. Perhaps he will tell you which restaurants are featuring live music of the type you prefer. And when you go to these restaurants there is always the chance that the band will play one of the songs you have learned. When they see you singing along they will be amazed and they will be happy to get to know you a little bit or perhaps invite you up onto the stage to sing with them.

As your knowledge of their music deepens, you will be able to enter, gradually, into the world of emotional expressions which are played and felt by the culture of which you are now becoming a part. In Middle Eastern music, as played in the Arab and Turkish world, there are many dozens of "maqamat" or "modes" or "scales" which carry differing emotional content. One scale will be associated with the loneliness of the night far out in the desert while another will be associated with Sufi mysticism. There are notes which our Western music doesn't even have which exist "between the keys on the piano," like B half-flats and F half-sharps. Hearing these notes will open new neural pathways. As you learn to play and sing in these different modes you will gain access to the emotions associated in that culture. This happens more and more directly when you begin playing with musicians over there. And playing music with people from all over the world is very much the same as having love affairs with them...

Anyone interested in studying the scales used in Arabic music can take advantage of many teaching materials now available including one that I wrote called "Basic Maqam Teachings." It consists of one book and two CDs and can be ordered from the www.musicalmissions.com website.

This man fabricates and plays ouds in Aleppo, in northern Syria.
I speak a little Arabic.
He speaks a little English.
We both speak Arabic music on the oud.

Becoming a Musical Ambassador

Spending time with a skilled musician-craftsman in Aleppo, Syria... this is the Magnification of the Heart... this is the gift of international love and friendship which comes with learning to open channels beyond verbal communication.

If we have charged our souls by balancing our personal habits so that our compassion can begin to flow, we may choose to become Musical Ambassadors, or "Musical Missionaries." As I say, we are being "missionaries in reverse" because we are not setting forth to teach. We have come to the realization that the gift of a compassionate heart is worth more than anything else. So we are on the road to learn and to give the gift of our hearts. There are very few Americans currently on the road in the Arab World. In five months of travel during 2002 & 2003, Kristina and I could count on the fingers of our hands the total number of American citizens we have met. During our first two months of travel in Jordan and the West Bank we saw none at all!

But it seems essential that more Americans realize that we can be the fore-runners of a new wave of people motivated not by fear, but by hope and by love. We are primed for sacred flirtation with the whole of humanity.

People who live in the more tropical lands are already on this wavelength. They have not been driven into materialistic ways of being by harsh cold winters. They have retained deep connections with their communities because they did not experience the loneliness and isolation of the nuclear family farm. That lifestyle may be responsible for much of the violence, not only between men and women, but between any kinds of "us and them."

As "Musical Ambassadors" in the 21st century we can learn to reclaim our universal sisterhoods and brotherhoods so that those who would rule by fear shall become obsolete and be seen as the ridiculously self-limiting energies that they are.

You don't have to be a musician in order to become a Musical Ambassador. All you need to do is find someone from the exotic part of the world to which you would like to go and have them recommend or provide a CD or a tape of a song which is extremely popular in their home country. Suggest that it be a love song. Most songs are love songs of one sort or another anyway. Once you have this song in your possession, listen to it a few times. Become familiar with the melody. See if there is a part of the song which functions as a "chorus" in that it is repeated frequently in the song. Try humming along with this chorus. It doesn't really matter whether you think of yourself as a singer or not. Everyone can at least make enthusiastic croaking sounds which could become recognizable as the chorus of a popular song. Lots of native people sing very enthusiastically off-key. Be off-key if necessary. Who knows, maybe later you will find more correct pitches. But it's your enthusiasm that counts!

Now you need to know what those few words are which go along with that chorus. The tape or cd may have lyrics printed in the insert which accompanies it. Some inserts actually give a transliteration and a translation both so that English-speaking audiences can easily know what the song is about. But your friend who initially recommended the song can help you with this. He or she may not understand your motivation, but be persistent until you can say and sing (or croak) this 5 to 15 second long piece of music! Buy yourself one or two inexpensive language learning programs at the bookstore at the same time and expose yourself to a little bit more of the language.

Now you are ready to climb on the airplane!

Now you are ready to land in the foreign culture of your choice and discover that, with a little more time and exploration, you have become a global citizen. What a relief! Not only are you on the road to incredible personal growth and expansion, but you are what the world most desperately needs: North Americans willing to join the rest of the planet!

Staying in inexpensive family-run hotels can be great spring-boards into a social life in a new city or village.

Expensive hotels unconsciously project strong divisive messages. As their "guest" you will be "protected" from the ordinary people who live in the surrounding areas unless you sign up for one of their expensive tours. And even if you sign up, you will still be "protected." You will be told that it is "dangerous" to leave the circle of their "protection." But do whatever you must do to get out of this trap and get your feet on the ground.

Any excuse for an outing will do. Take some photos and find a film-developing shop. Strike up friendships with the people who work there. Take the photos, perhaps along with some photos from your own hometown and family, and show them to the waiter in an inexpensive restaurant. Make sure that you frequent restaurants where the local folks eat too. If you simply visit the places where all the tourists go, you'll never get out of the cage.

By eating in a variety of places, as long as the food tastes good and fresh, you are actually exercising your immune system and your long term health will show increased stamina and strength! The current wave of "immune system disorders" here in America is probably because we don't expose ourselves to enough "dirt." Doctors from India, perplexed at the fragility of the North

American immune system, have done studies which show that this is true.

Begin experimenting with your song. Hopefully your friend did help you select a truly popular song which everyone knows. If not, learn another one. Try humming the tune in a taxi cab. Hum it to the waitress. Hum in on the bus. When you find the people who recognize it, don't be surprised if they invite you to visit them or their aunts and uncles.

Say "yes" when these invitations come. If you don't say "yes" then what's the point? Of course you will hear lots of fear-based advice from fellow Americans. Lots of reasons will be offered about why you should say "no." Re-read the chapter called "you are safer over there" if you must.

Seriously, in all the places I have been, the only dangers I have ever encountered have been from drunk off-duty law-enforcement officials in alcohol-oriented Western countries. Avoid those particular individuals.

Women certainly are in a more vulnerable position than I, as a male. There are times when a woman's internal radar tells her to say "no" and she should follow that instinct. But, after a period of familiarization with the local culture, she may find that she doesn't have to say "no" very often.

If you are in the Muslim world, then you really don't have to worry so much because people don't (outside of the super-wealthy classes and the tourist resorts and towns) drink alcohol. Their passion is for offering tea and hospitality and exchanging friendship. At first it may seem hard to believe, because we are a little more reluctant to offer hospitality in America, especially to foreigners. But believe it! It's really true!

Whatever happens to you while carrying out these Musical Missions will be a step in the right direction. I guarantee it won't take long before you begin to feel membership in an extended global community. Go and visit music stores. Sing your song with the salesmen who vend the tapes and CDs. That's a sure bet. And if they recommend some other tape or CD, buy it! Learn something from it and return a few days later to sing for them a little bit.

Keep on the path. Your efforts will bring fruits which will multiply: new friendships based on nothing more nor less than a song! In a friendship such as this there is nothing to trust or mistrust. Whatever is happening can be taken at face value. There are no ulterior motives. Sharing of heart energies is what it's all about!

Inca elders in Cuzco, Peru.

Learning to Become
Responsible Global Citizens

As contemporary adults on planet earth we have the challenge of creating a new Global Democracy. In this new world order people of all races will feel equal and free. Some nations may chose to select leaders in ways that are different from our American system. It appears to me that Arab-world people might prefer to invest power in Muslim leaders. If they feel connected to the most enlightened possible leadership that way, then they will feel free to make such choices. Eventually, an evolved humanity stands a chance of living once again in a world without borders.

EYE CONTACT

People in the Arab-speaking world have a very obvious and fascinating way of communicating: while they are having a conversation with you, they look continuously deeply into your soul from very close up. And they allow you to look deeply into their souls at the same time.

We all know what it means to feel that the eyes are windows into the soul. Here in America we also look deeply into each other's souls through our eyes. (When we're not wearing sunglasses, that is.) We can see the textures of our emotions in each other's eyes.

How exactly this works we do not really understand. But deep eye contact and the reading of other types of body language enable us to feel that we know a lot about a person before we have done any more than simply pass them on the street or buy a cup of tea from them.

Here in America we have a slightly different habit: unless we know someone extremely well, we feel the need, after 15 seconds or so of eye contact, to look away. And many of us don't know how to comfortably look with both eyes simultaneously – left eye to right eye and right eye to left eye – and maintain an unbroken channel of eye communication. It is more common for us Americans, when we do maintain eye contact, to alternate looking from one of the other person's eyes to the other, rapidly changing our focus back and forth. This actually causes little interruptions in eye communication although we are not usually aware of this. It is not until we learn from people from other parts of the world how to maintain continual and balanced eye communication – left eye to right eye and right eye to left eye – that we even know what we are missing. We are, as a culture, "shifty" by comparison. It is almost impossible to lie to someone while maintaining a truly deep and balanced continual eye contact.

JUSTICE AND THE POLITICS OF FEAR

Interestingly, our legal system may be evolving in a similarly "shifty" way. Are our legal battles turning more toward getting people convicted or acquitted on "technicalities" than toward straight-forward evaluation of honor and justice?

Arab-world citizens are more accustomed to thinking of justice in more absolute ways especially since Islam is a religion which was intended to be a complete social code defining the "right ways" from the "wrong ways" of doing things. This, as we all know, can have its drawbacks. Societies continue to evolve. New situations defy interpretation according to old codes of "good and evil." And the very idea of preserving a "sacred text," as we linguists know, is destined for confusion because languages evolve so rapidly. This requires frequent re-translation of the original "sacred" documents and the original meanings can get replaced by new wordings which not only obscure the original intent but create new definitions of "good and evil." Cleverly buried advantages within the new "slanted" descriptions enhance subtle political powers for newly evolving classes of people or for certain biased rulers.

But still, it seems to me possible that Arab World citizens would sooner trust a leader with whom they can establish and maintain deep eye-contact than one whose credentials rest with having connections to the governments of the West.

Our Western politicians are, for the most part, reflecting the bottom line of fear-driven reality. It has become a politics of fear rather than a politics of hope. Less materialistic societies would not feel well-represented by such governments, although politicians scrambling for popular votes might find that their best chance for election would lie in sowing seeds of fear in the populace and then making promises to "protect" them. It's really the same old "protection" racquet practiced in gangland-controlled neighborhoods.

We, the people, have to use our courage, our ecstasy and our inspiration and our love and our hearts to retake the reins of the path of human growth and steer us into creativity before the powers of destruction can erupt... again...

Do we really want to
waste this precious lifetime?

What skills do we have? What does it seem that the world most needs? How can we proceed rapidly toward fully engaging our own primal creativity?

In order to do the hope and love-driven work that the politicians usually cannot afford the time to pursue, we have to begin changing some old habits which are focused on giving us security. After all, what is security? It is based on fear. Why would we want to live lives based on fear?

And then the prophet said,
"I won't drink from another cup with these poor people
until I receive my health insurance policy in the mail!"

Don't we all yearn to be so involved with *generosity* that fear of death is a relatively minor concern? If great healers were driven by fears of their own deaths they certainly wouldn't hang out around all those disease-ridden beggars!

Did the divine meditator wait to sit down under that tree until he was sure he could afford to? Or did he sit down there when he was convinced that he could not afford not to?

As time slips by, we look for moments when we can make our move: we can move away from materially-rewarded life styles into love-rewarded life styles. Perhaps this is only the first step toward a life driven by some rewards we cannot yet fathom, but we must take this step when we can. And we must realize that circumstances will never provide a "perfect moment" for this.

We will have to accept some uncertainty about what the future will bring. We must trade some material security for a spiritual adventure which is in harmony with all of humanity. The choices are ours to make.

Endnotes:

[1] *In An Antique Land, History in the Guise of a Traveler's Tale,* by the Indian anthropologist, Amitav Ghosh   Originally published in 1992 by Alfred A. Knopf

[2] Excerpts from the beginning of Chapter 4 of Imam Feisal Abdul Rauf's fascinating book: *What's Right with Islam,* Published in 2004 by HarperCollins. He is an Imam from Kuwait who is the head of one of New York City's largest mosques.

[3] *A Song for One or Two: Music and the Concept of Art in Early China,* Author: Kenneth J. DeWoskin Published 1982 by the Center for Chinese Studies, University of Michigan

[4] *Traffickers' New Cargo: Naive Slavic Women,* Michael Specter, New York Times, January 11, 1998.

[5] *In An Antique Land, History in the Guise of a Traveler's Tale* by the Indian anthropologist, Amitav Ghosh
Originally published in 1992 by Alfred A. Knopf

[6] *The Scimitar and the Veil,* Jennifer Heath, Published by Hidden Spring, 2004, P 171

Poem

Tomatoes

cucumbers and foxes are out late tonight...
turn off the tv... go out and explore... it's your life they're stealing!
gravel in the pond... peaches in the orchard... it's your choice!
life is not that movie we just saw...
that was a lie...

please come to the table with yourself and your brother...
don't fall off the cliff!

it's happening here beside the stream...
it's happening here where the water flows into spiral space...
it's definitely happening here where the tomatoes are glowing red!
where the curtains blow over your bed...
where the driveway enters your house...
oh my god! don't lose track of it now! it really is your life!

surrounded by suspicions... surrounded by low-life bottom-dwellers...
don't take the poison!
remember to scream through the rapids
in your own bright orange boat...

the danger in the wilderness...
it's not in your mind: it's in someone else's mind!
don't believe a word of it!
go out and explore!
there's only so much time...
the curtains of fear are being sold at low prices...

find your mates... they all love you!
pomegranates for friends... they will never betray you!

check it out! it's all right here on the street where you live!
don't miss the brown babies floating down the Amazon...
don't forget the sweet song from the African survival!
caress an Arab's hand...
don't forget the Eskimos...
watch out how the hours are spent!
come on my friend, I'm rooting for you!

every ounce of heaven was made for you and me...
video game fraud... Hollywood heaven... will steal your brain!
Aphrodite is down beside the pool, waiting for her man...
did you get a whiff of her smell?
don't ever forget it!
you can't smell her through the television screen...

oh soul of modern world I cry for you
when the damsel tells a tale of plastic...
and forsakes her own tenuous dreams...
please, put the clouds back in the sky!
put the grapes back on the vine!
put the silk back on your breast!
put the feathers back on that bird of paradise!
don't you dare go to your grave without finding it!
it's yours it's yours! it's yours for the taking!
it's yours for the believing!

give it a soul a dark velvet soul... look into the eyes and find it there...
hearts are made for your sweet tongue!
don't miss this chance! don't neglect this dance!
you already are a superhero!
you are naked in your smooth olive oil...
it's never too soon and it's never too late...

the violin is listening to join the tune...
all you need is to supply the fingers and the bow....
someone is trying to highjack your sweet reflection in the pond!
don't choose fear!
or you'll have to pay with cascades of giddy waterfalls of disease...
not for you my sweet one!

yes, there is some loneliness for you to curl up into...
it is the embrace of the goddess....

don't pollute the tugging on your heart with the lies told in the news...
walk the gardens of Babylon...
go into Iraq and greet the sweet people!
learn their ancient song!
boldly forward into the marketplace
we carry our music high above our heads!
we feel the power of the crowd...

airplanes have left the skies for now and made a space for song...
the dead are dead and you and I are still living!
live your dance! create your romance!
forsake your living room and go out into the garden....
the gods, the little ones and the great ones... are waiting...
"hello" they will say to you in greeting...
"thank god you found the path!"
this life is for you! my sweet goddess...
you with the strawberries in your basket...

now all that is required is that we live and die with honor!
don't worry... honor knows what that means...
honor is your friend and will guide you through the gates...
never trust an over-full stomach...
we don't really need more sleep....
only rest... yes we do need rest...

branches are blooming above us...
have you recently talked about this with the birds?
don't be silly! of course they know about these things!

that brings us to the canyon's rim... where the redness turns to gold...
the blue sky cradles the white stars
as the winds of night blow through your hair...
the waters know which way to go...
so do you... with that scarf of silk around your neck...
with that leather saddle between your legs....
there is a promised land... funny thing: it's right here!

don't miss out on the Peruvians: sweet and ancient people...
if you haven't been to China, buy a ticket...
go to the places where they sell the tomatoes...
these are the sacred spots for today...

forget the cathedrals and their glory...
don't worry, they had their day...
they were alive in their time...
how exciting it was when the last stone was put into place...
but that was yesteryear... and now they will fill your soul with dust...
you will feel a strange museum-fatigue creeping into you...
let them die... it's only a fair kindness... yes! now you must go
to where the tomatoes
are being sold by those men and those women...
you must look into their eyes...
you must say "tomato" in seventeen tongues...
you must prostrate yourself before the tomato man...
and you must enter the path of your own life!
forget the news! forget the war!
forget governments and their rackets...
beyond it all you will find the tomato ladies
and you will enter a golden heaven...
walk the streets behind the market...
the smell of urine an ancient perfume...
diesel engines idle beside the resting donkey...
those peas have come through many hands to make it to downtown...
don't worry... no one ever starves to death here...

if you have time, go again the next day... and the next...
out there in the market, check out the cucumbers...
they were recently washed!
check out the squash amaranth cilantro parsley onion apple luxury...
something holy is happening here!
the CNN cameras are strangely absent!
they are doggedly pursuing terror...
but we are all over here... admiring the tomato...
ok... I'm going to buy that one there!
shukran, gracias, efharisto... danka, merci, spasiba...
teshekur ederim, yusulpayki, yes, thank you!
I've got to go! But I think I'll be back tomorrow....

Something about this place...
Something about your face... maybe we're in love...
Back in the hotel the waiters look at me with dollar bills in their eyes...
Disgusted, I check out into the streets...
I wander until I find the man....
I wander until I find that land...
I wander until her heart melts into mine and my resting place is safe...
My song blends into the midnight call to prayer...

early patches of dawn bathe the sleeping village....
picking up where we left off,
we discover that the children have been born...
the dust beneath your footstep is a soft blessing
as you wash your clothes...
the machine gun fire in the distance cannot harm you now...
it is only dangerous for the ones who are still watching the tv...
the musician is never shot while singing his song...
go down by the river... cars and trucks and buses and trolleys...
further down by the river....
trash and broken concrete... the smell of hot tar...
no, further down by the river...
where the water runs...
there...

Fresh Vegetables in Jordan!

Itinerary of Musical Missions
2002 – 2004

Here is a list of some of the places in which we have done our concerts, presentations, workshops and interviews between the fall of 2002 and the fall of 2004:

Baghdad, Iraq; Cairo, Egypt; Damascus, Syria; Amman, Jordan; Aleppo, Syria; Lattakia, Syria, Ramallah, West Bank; Aqaba, Jordan; Sandia Park, NM; Long Beach, CA; Monterey, CA; Santa Cruz, CA; Ashland, OR; Bolinas, CA; Santa Barbara, CA; Denver, CO; Wolcott, CO; Westminster, CO; Golden, CO; Albuquerque, NM; Grand Junction, CO; Abiquiu, NM; Santa Fe, NM; Fort Worth, TX; Denton, TX; Fayetteville, AR; Lacombe, LA; New Orleans, LA; Slidell, LA; Mobile, AL; Columbus, GA; Durham, NC; Chattanooga, TN; Summertown, TN; Cookeville, TN; Nashville, TN; Estes Park, CO; Lafayette, CO; Dillon, CO; Frisco, CO; Avon, CO; Hillsboro, OR; Klamath Falls, OR; Corvallis, OR; Berkeley, CA; Oakland, CA; Laguna Beach, CA; Costa Mesa, CA; Mission Viejo, CA; Sonora, CA; Eugene, OR; Grants Pass, OR; Milwaukie, OR; Port Angeles, WA; Chelan, WA; Yakima, WA; Pocatello, ID; Idaho Falls, ID; Ft. Collins, CO; Lakewood, CO; Northglenn, CO; Del Norte, CO; Crestone, CO; Basalt, CO; Kansas City, KS; Rolla, MO; Terre Haute, IN; Bean Blossom, IN; Allentown, PA; Jonestown, PA; Flint, MI; Cincinnati, OH; Brattleboro, VT; Pottersville, NJ; Farmingdale, NY; Edinboro, PA; Racine, WI; Peoria, IL; Rockford, IL; West Lafayette, IN; Mankato, MN; Des Moines, IA; and, of course, our home town of Boulder, CO.

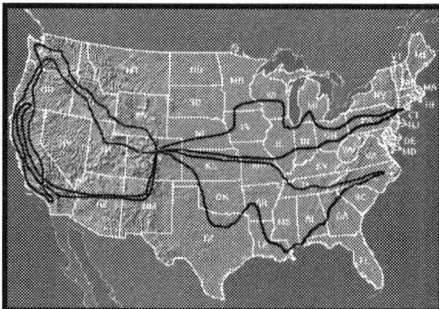

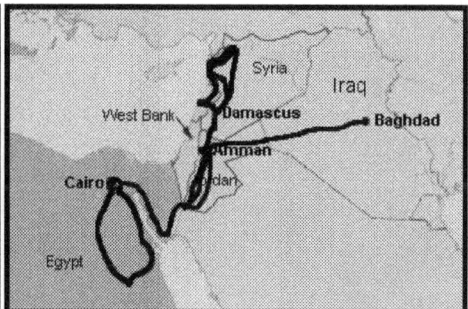

Other Books by Cameron Powers:
Published by GL Design

Singing in Baghdad
A Musical Mission of Peace

Singing in Baghdad: A Musical Mission of Peace, 2nd Edition
ISBN/SKU:0-9745882-5-3
ISBN Complete: 978-0-9745882-5-4
Publication Date: 12-05-2005
Selling Price: $16.95 USD
(plus $4 shipping and handling)

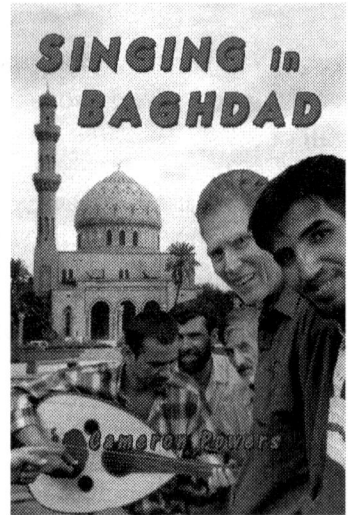

A real-life modern Musical Mission of Peace into Baghdad: American couple put their hearts on the line and invade Iraq by singing popular Arabic music on the streets of Baghdad as the US Marines invade with weaponry in the spring of 2003. They give another message to Iraqi people: we're here to sing and to learn and to listen. How were they received? And what was it like for them in the streets of Cairo, Ramallah, Amman and other Arab cities armed only with their singing voices and an Oud, an ancient Arabic lute? This is a fantastic view into the hearts and minds of the Arab world unparalleled and unique in modern reporting.

Arabic Musical Scales: Basic Maqam Teachings

Book and two audio CDs
ISBN/SKU: 0-9745882-3-7
ISBN Complete: 978-0-9745882-3-0
Publication Date: 12-05-2005
Price: $34.95 (plus $4 shipping and handling)

This comprehensive book and CD set includes 45 scales for the musician interested in learning to play Near Eastern dance music, sacred music, or folk music.

From Cairo to Tunisia, Damascus to Baghdad, Beirut to Aleppo, and as far west as Istanbul and Greece, musicians live and breathe these ancient scales, which have survived intact for hundreds, and in some cases, thousands of years.

Anyone interested in micro-tonal musical intervals would do well to dip into this ancient tradition.

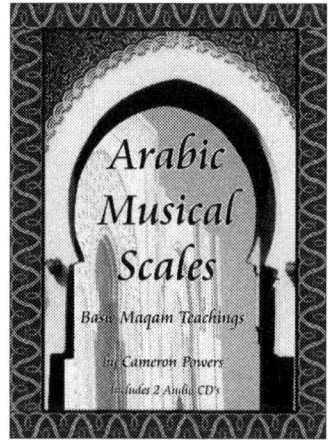

Additional copies of *Spiritual Traveler* or the books listed above can be ordered at:

Website: http://www.gldesignpub.com
or E-Mail: distrib@gldesign.com

Or send check of money order to:
GL Design
2090 Grape Ave
Boulder, CO 80304   USA

For more information visit: http://www.musicalmissions.com